Longman Pocket Companion Series

Pocket Companion

Musical Quotes
and
Anecdotes

Longman

Foreword

Music is one of the great joys of life. There is nothing quite like it. I cannot think of a time when I didn't like it. I think I loved it from the very first moment when I heard music on the radio or was taken to hear bands play in the park. The attempt to capture the quality of music by writing about it in words is doomed to failure. The task is essentially impossible. Music is music. It is what it is. The experience cannot be rendered in any other terms. Nevertheless, many have tried to describe it, or to recapture or preserve musical experiences in terms of language. Some have succeeded brilliantly – Bernard Shaw and Neville Cardus are quite rightly among the immortals in this respect.

Journals, biographies, diaries, plays, novels and anecdotes all contain fascinating evidence of the attempt to convey the experience of music verbally. Not all this writing is of high literary merit, but it is all of interest to those to whom music means something. This book is an attempt to bring together a fair sample of my favourite writing about music. W.H. Auden once wrote: 'Aside from purely technical analysis, nothing can be *said* about music, except when it is bad; when it is good, one can only listen and be grateful.' In some ways, this book is an attempt to prove Auden wrong. I think it is true that very often a writer is able to convey personal distaste for certain kinds of music very effectively (Ruskin's dictum on Beethoven's music, 'like the upsetting of a bag of nails, with here and there an also dropped hammer') and that musical approval is difficult to express without descent into the gushing. In spite of all this, I dedicate this book to the belief that good writing about music is possible.

Next to listening to music I love reading about it. I hope this book falls into the hands of fellow spirits.

Robert Giddings
February 1984

Amateur Musicians

'Said Oscar Wilde: "Each man kills the thing he loves".
For example, the amateur musician.'

H.L. Mencken (1880–1956)

Auden, W.H. (1907–73)

'If music in general is an imitation of history, opera in
particular is an imitation of human wilfulness; it is rooted
in the fact that we not only have feelings but insist upon
having them at whatever cost to ourselves. Opera,
therefore, cannot present character in the novelist's
sense of the word, namely, people who are potentially
good *and* bad, active *and* passive, for music is immediate
actuality and neither potentiality nor passivity can live in
its presence. . . .

The quality common to all the great operatic roles,
e.g., Don Giovanni, Norma, Lucia, Tristan, Isolde,
Brünnhilde, is that each of them is a passionate and
wilful state of being. In real life they would all be bores,
even Don Giovanni.

In recompense for this lack of psychological complexity, however, music can do what words cannot,
present the immediate and simultaneous relation of
these states to each other. The crowning glory of opera is
the big ensemble.'

W.H. Auden 'Notes on Music and Opera' in *The Dyer's
Hand and Other Essays* (1962)

Audiences

'Because I have no ear for music, at the concert of the
Quintette Club, it looked to me as if the performers were
crazy, and all the audience were make-believe crazy, in
order to soothe the lunatics and keep them amused.'

Ralph Waldo Emerson (1803–82) *Journals*

'Yesterday was *Don Giovanni* under Wagner, with an
overflowing house but a most dull, stupid and thankless
audience. Wagner had taken the most exceptional
trouble, and we had all three been several days and
nights correcting errors in the orchestral parts, replacing
instruments which were lacking, such as trombones,
with others. Wagner had translated the Italian recitatives
into German – he also simplified the scenery, and had
cleverly reduced the everlasting scene-changing to a
single one in the first act. . . . It has driven me nearly wild
when I remember how Wagner used to be accused in
Dresden of conducting Mozart's music badly on purpose

– how he could not bear his music because he was so eaten up by his own conceit. . . .'

Hans von Bülow, in a letter to his father, from Zurich, Oct 1850

'Tonight I heard Yvette Guilbert sing five songs – including "La Soularde", Beranger's "Grand'mère", "Her Golden Hair was hanging down her back" and "I want you, ma Honey" (alternate verses in French and English). The performance took about twenty five minutes, and she receives £70 per night (ten nights). My father, who had seen her on the previous evening, said to me at dinner at Gatti's:

"I don't see £70 in what she does."

"No," I said, "perhaps *you* can't; but you can see it in the audience which pays to listen to her."

I think I never saw the Empire so full. . . .'

Arnold Bennett *Journals*, entry for 8 May 1896

'The concert began with Mozart's G Minor Symphony. We liked this fairly well, especially the last movement, but we found all the movements too long . . . if each movement had been half as long I should probably have felt cordially enough towards it. . . .

Then came a terribly long-winded recitative by Beethoven and an air with a good deal of "Che farò" in it. I do not mind this, and if it had been "Che farò" absolutely I should, I daresay, have liked it better. I never want to hear it again. . . .

Beethoven's Concerto for violin and orchestra which followed was longer and more tedious still. I have not a single good word for it. . . .

Part II opened with a Suite in F Major for orchestra by Moszkoski. This was much more clear and, in every way, interesting than Beethoven; every now and then there were passages that were pleasing, not to say more . . . one could not feel that any of the movements were the mere drivelling show stuff of which the Concerto had been full. But it, like everything else down at these concerts, is too long, cut down one half it would have been all right and we should have liked to hear it twice. As it was, all we could say was that it was much better than we had expected. I did not like the look of the young man who wrote it and who also conducted. He had long yellowish hair and kept tossing his head to fling it back on to his shoulders, instead of keeping it short as Jones and I keep ours.'

Samuel Butler *Note Books* (1912)

In *Three Men in a Boat* there is a description of a musical evening at a party, which, as the author admits: 'throws much light upon the inner mental workings of human nature in general'. This 'fashionable and highly cultured' group listen to odds and ends from the classics, discuss ethics, listen to poetry:

'Somebody recited a French poem ... we said it was beautiful; and then a lady sang a sentimental ballad in Spanish, and it made one or two of us weep ...' and then two young students, who had just returned from Germany, recommended that they listen to the great German comic song, rendered by a fellow-guest, Herr Slossenn Boschen.

'Herr Slossenn Boschen accompanied himself. The prelude did not suggest a comic song exactly. It was a weird, soulful air. It quite made one's flesh creep; but we murmured ... that it was the German method, and prepared to enjoy it.

I don't understand German myself. I learned it at school, but forgot every word of it two years after I had left, and have felt much better ever since. Still I did not want the people there to guess my ignorance; so I hit upon what I thought to be rather a good idea. I kept my eye on the two young students, and followed them. When they tittered, I tittered; when they roared, I roared; and I also threw in a little snigger all by myself now and then, as if I had seen a bit of humour that had escaped the others. I considered this particularly artful on my part.

... other people also tittered when the young men tittered, and roared when the young men roared; and, as the two young men tittered and roared and exploded with laughter pretty continuously all through the song, it went exceedingly well.

And yet that German professor did not seem happy. At first, when we began to laugh the expression of his face was one of intense surprise, as if laughter were the very last thing he had expected. . . . We thought this very funny; we said his earnest manner was half the humour. The slightest hint on his part that he knew how funny he was would have completely ruined it all. As we continued to laugh, his surprise gave way to an air of annoyance and indignation, and he scowled fiercely round upon us all. . . . That sent us into convulsions. We told each other that it would be the death of us, this thing. The words alone, we said, were enough to send us into fits, but added to his mock seriousness – oh, it was too much!

In the last verse, he surpassed himself. He glowered round upon us with a look of such concentrated ferocity that, but for our being forewarned as to the German method of comic singing, we should have been nervous; and he threw such a wailing note of agony into the weird music that, if we had not known it was a funny song, we might have wept.

He finished amid a perfect shriek of laughter.'

They believed it was the funniest thing they had ever heard and said how strange it was that there was a popular belief that the 'Germans hadn't any sense of humour'. They asked Herr Slossenn Boschen why he didn't translate the song into English, 'so that the common people could understand it, and hear what a real comic song was like'. The professor was furious: 'It appeared that the song was not a comic song at all. It was about a young girl who lived in the Hartz Mountains, and who had given up her life to save her lover's soul; and he died, and met her spirit in the air; and then, in the last verse, he jilted her spirit and went off with another spirit – I'm not quite sure of the details, but it was something very sad, I know.... He (Herr Boschen) said it was generally acknowledged to be one of the most tragic and pathetic songs in the German language.

It was a trying situation for us – very trying. There seemed to be no answer. We looked round for the two young men ... but they had left the house in an unostentatious manner.... That was the end of the party. I never saw a party break up so quietly....'

Jerome K. Jerome *Three Men in a Boat* (1889)

'Last year, more Americans went to symphonies [symphony concerts] than went to baseball games. This may be viewed as an alarming statistic, but I think that both baseball and the country will endure.'

John F. Kennedy, during a speech at a White House Youth Concert, 6 Aug 1962; in **Bill Adler** ed *The Kennedy Wit* (1964)

'That reminds me. I'm playing a concert tonight.'

Fritz Kreisler (1875–1962) on viewing rows of fish lying on a fishmonger's slab

'Playing music in America you feel you're selling a luxury item. But in England you're providing a necessity.'

Isaac Stern, in an interview with **John Mortimer**, in *The Sunday Times* (20 March 1983)

Bach, Johann Sebastian (1685–1750)

'... anything which will enhance the natural beauty of the work, or the plastic value of the performance, anything which will add vigour or delicacy to it, is not only allowed but actually demanded by the score. If Bach had had our resources at his disposal he would have used them in this way.... We can only ''modernise'' Bach. If we perform his works as they were in his day they would not make the same impression on the modern listener, since he is much more exacting than the faithful of St. Thomas Church.'

Albert Schweitzer *J.S. Bach, Musician and Poet* (1911)

'The miracle of Bach has not appeared in any other art. To strip human nature until its divine attributes are made clear, to inform ordinary activities with spiritual fervour, to give wings of eternity to that which is most ephemeral; to make divine things human and human things divine; such is Bach, the greatest and purest moment in music of all time.'

Pablo Casals, in **J.M. Corredor** *Conversations with Casals* (1956)

'In order to understand a great composer and to perform his works as they should be performed, it is important to know also the surroundings this composer lived in. In order to know these things (in regard to Bach) it becomes necessary to obliterate from our minds all the developments which took place after Bach, all the things which in his day had not been discovered, written or achieved. To understand Bach in his day we shall have therefore to forget all the music of Haydn, Mozart, Beethoven, all romanticism and also the philosophy of free thinking, the political and geographical conceptions of the generations subsequent to Bach. We shall have to imagine all the things which, as far as we are concerned, have disappeared in the past, but were active and visible in his day; the religious habits of his century, his symbolism, his connection with the Church. Only thus, shall we understand the Master, not just through ourselves, but objectively.'

Edwin Fischer *Johann Sebastian Bach* (Berne, 1948)

'Mozart begins by charming our ears in a most delicious way and then gives our body and soul an indescribable feeling of well-being. Bach lifts the soul away from the body. Without trying to maintain a paradox, we can say that in spite of his austerity and the greater age of his forms, Bach is more modern than Mozart.'

William Cart *J.S. Bach 1685–1753*

Bagpipes

Each roared with throat at widest stretch
For Will the Piper–low born wretch!
Will forward steps, as best he can,
Unlike a free, ennobled man;
A pliant bag 'tween arm and chest,
While limping on, he tightly prest,
He stares – he strives the bag to sound;
He swells his maw – and ogles round;
He twists and turns himself about –
With fetid breath his cheeks swell out.
The churl did blow a grating shriek,
The bag did swell and harshly squeak,

As does a goose from nightmare crying,
Or dog, crushed by a chest when dying;
This whistling box's changeless note
Is forced from turgid veins and throat;
Its sound is like a crane's harsh moan,
Or like a gosling's latest groan;
Just such a noise a wounded goat
Sends forth from her hoarse and gurgling throat.

Lewis Glyn Cothi (died 1486), describing a Saxon
wedding in his poem *The Saxons of Flint*

Some men there are that love not a gaping pig;
Some, that are mad if they behold a cat;
And others, when the bagpipe sings i' the nose,
Cannot contain their urine . . .

William Shakespeare *The Merchant of Venice*, Act IV,
scene i (1596)

'We had the music of the bagpipe every day, at Ar-
midale, Dunvegan, and Col. Dr. Johnson appeared fond
of it, and used often to stand for some time with his ear
close to the great drone.'

James Boswell *Journal of a Tour to the Hebrides* (1785)

Let me play to you tunes without measure or end,
Tunes that are born to die without a herald,
As a flight of storks rises from a marsh, circles,
And alights on the spot from which it rose.

Flowers. A flower-bed like hearing the bagpipes.
The fine black earth has clotted into sharp masses
As if the frost and not the sun had come.
It holds many lines of flowers.
First faint rose peonies, then peonies blushing,
Then again red peonies, and behind them,
Massive, apoplectic peonies, some of which are so red
And so violent as to seem almost black; behind these
Stands a low hedge of larkspur, whose tender
    apologetic blossoms
Appear by contrast pale, though some, vivid as the sky
    above them,
Stand out from their fellows, iridescent and slaty as a
    pigeon's breast.
The bagpipes – they are screaming and they
    are sorrowful.
There is a wail in their merriment, and cruelty in
    their triumph.
They rise and they fall like a weight swung in the air at
    the end of a string.
They are like the red blood of those peonies.
And like the melancholy of those blue flowers.
They are like a human voice – no! for the human
    voice lies!

They are like human life that flows under the words.
That flower-bed is like the true life that wants to
    express itself
And does . . . while we human beings lie cramped
    and fearful.

Hugh MacDiarmid *Bagpipe Music* (1943)

Barbirolli, Sir John (1899–1970)

Two concert-goers were walking down Denmark Street
in London. They passed a poster which announced:

> THE HALLE ORCHESTRA
>
> *conducted by*
>
> Sir John Barbirolli

They walked on past another poster which read:

> THE HALLE
> STRING ORCHESTRA
>
> *conducted by*
>
> Sir John Barbirolli

A few yards further on they came to a poster which
advertised a concert by

> THE BARBIROLLI
> STRING QUARTET

One looked at the other and said: 'We'd better go and
hear this outfit before it folds up.'

In 1936 Barbirolli was appointed conductor of the
Philharmonic–Symphony Orchestra of New York in
succession to Arturo Toscanini. After six months Toscanini returned to conduct a concert; he said to Barbirolli:
'John, my orchestra is just as I left it'. Barbirolli's contract
was then renewed for a further two years.

Quoted in **Donald Brook** *Conductors' Gallery* (1947)

'I always have a boiled egg. A three-minute egg. Do you
know how I time it? I bring it to the boil and then conduct
the Overture to *The Marriage of Figaro*. Three minutes
exactly.'

Sir John Barbirolli, in an interview for the BBC radio
programme *Woman's Hour*

Bartók, Béla (1881–1945)

'If the reader were so rash as to purchase any of Béla Bartók's compositions, he would find that they each and all consist of unmeaning bunches of notes, apparently representing the composer promenading the keyboard in his boots. Some can be played better with the elbows, others with the flat of the hand. None require fingers to perform nor ears to listen to.'

Musical Quarterly 1 (1915)

The fourth movement ('Intermezzo interrotto') of Bartók's Concerto for Orchestra consists of a quiet, wandering melody which is interrupted by a coarse band-like section which gradually fades away; the haunting slow music returns, slightly changed, as the movement ends. The composer once asked the conductor, Antal Dorati: 'Do you know what the interruption in the fourth movement is?' Dorati answered: 'Oh yes!' 'Well, what is it?'

Dorati believed, as many musicians do, that this vulgar passage is a quotation, and he said: 'It is from Lehár's *Merry Widow*?' Bartók was extremely puzzled and asked: 'What is *that*?' In telling this story in his autobiography, Dorati concludes: 'Could it be that he didn't know Lehár, our countryman's, world famous operetta?

No. He didn't know it.

I gave up.

He said with a twinkle in his eye: "I will tell you what it is, but you must not tell anybody as long as I am alive."

I promised. (And I kept my word.)

"It is a parody of Shostakovich!"

And of course it was: very clearly audible, once one had been told, but I would never have spotted it. Then Bartók told me of his dislike for Shostakovich. He never said anything derogatory of anyone, especially not of another composer. This was a singular instance.'

Antal Dorati *Notes of Seven Decades* (1979)

Bass

With whisper of her mellowing grain,
With treble of brook and bud of tree,
Earth joys forever to sustain
The bass eternal of the sea.

Roden Noel *Beatrice*

Bass Drum

Berlioz describes the rapturous reception given to a new arrangement of his Rákóczy March, which features impressive use of the bass drum, when it was performed at Pest (in what is now Budapest), Hungary, in 1846:

'After a trumpet fanfare ... the theme ... is announced piano by flutes and clarinets accompanied by pizzicato strings. The audience remained calm and judicious during this unexpected exposition. But when a long crescendo ensued, with fragments of the theme reintroduced fugally, broken by the dull strokes of the bass drum, like the thud of distant cannon, the whole place began to stir and hum with excitement, and when the orchestra unleashed its full fury and the long-delayed fortissimo burst forth, a tumult of shouting and stamping shook the theatre; the accumulated pressure of all that seething mass of emotion exploded with a violence that sent a thrill of fear right through me. . . .'

The Memoirs of Hector Berlioz, translated and edited by David Cairns (1969)

Bax, Sir Arnold (1883–1953)

'Bax has endowed the orchestra with a magnificent library of works, all of them of great interest to play and many of them extremely difficult. . . . At rehearsals he is generally prowling around the back of the rostrum, aiding and abetting the conductor. Extraordinarily diffident and self-effacing, he never fusses the orchestra and he seldom changes his mind on his scoring, leaving all such matters to the conductor. The orchestra finds rehearsals trying when there are two minds in control, but Bax is generally only concerned with queries and matters of balance and *tempi*. He is never dictatorial, never touchy or irritable. . . . Many of Bax's works . . . are as thrilling to play as to listen to. . . .'

Bernard Shore *The Orchestra Speaks (1937)*

Bayreuth

'The great building stands all by itself, grand and lonely, on a high ground outside the town. . . . The interior of the building is simple – severely so; but there is no occasion for color and decoration, since the people sit in the dark. The auditorium has the shape of a keystone, with the stage at the narrow end. There is an aisle on each side, but no aisle in the body of the house. Each row of seats extends in an unbroken curve from one side of the house to the other. There are seven entrance doors on each side of the theater and four at the butt, eighteen doors to admit and emit 1,650 persons. The number of the particular door by which you are to enter the house or leave it is printed on your ticket, and you can use no door but that one. Thus, crowding and confusion are impossible. Not so many as a hundred people use any one door. This is better than having the usual (and useless) elaborate fireproof arrangements. It is the model theater of the world. It can be emptied while the second hand of a watch makes its circuit. It would be entirely safe, even if it were built of lucifer matches.

If your seat is near the center of a row and you enter late you must work your way along a rank of about twenty-five ladies and gentlemen to get to it. Yet this causes no trouble, for everybody stands up until all the seats are full, and the filling is accomplished in a very few minutes. Then all sit down, and you have a solid mass of fifteen hundred heads, making a steep cellar-door slant from the rear of the house down to the stage.

All the lights were turned low, so low that the congregation sat in deep and solemn gloom. The funereal rustling of dresses and the low buzz of conversation began to die swiftly down, and presently not the ghost of a sound was left. This profound and increasingly impressive stillness endured for some time – the best preparation for music, spectacle, or speech conceivable. I should think our show people would have invented or imported that simple and impressive device for securing and solidifying the attention of an audience long ago; instead of which they continue to this day to open a performance against a deadly competition in the form of noise, confusion, and a scattered interest.

Finally, out of darkness and distance and mystery soft rich notes rose upon the stillness, and from his grave the dead magician began to weave his spells about his disciples and steep their souls in his enchantment. There was something strangely impressive in the fancy which kept intruding itself that the composer was conscious in his grave of what was going on here, and that these divine sounds were the clothing of thoughts which were at this moment passing through his brain, and not recognized and familiar ones which had issued from it at some former time.'

Mark Twain, recounting a visit to the Bayreuth Festival in 1891, in At the Shrine of St. Wagner, *New York Sun* (1891)

Beecham, Sir Thomas (1879–1961)

During the bankruptcy proceedings in which Beecham found himself after the First World War it was mentioned that he had spent a very considerable part of his private fortune providing good music for the edification of the British public. The learned judge remarked at this: 'What's the good of that?' Later in the proceedings a reference was made to 'the musical profession'. Another member of the legal profession then asked: 'You don't call that a profession, do you?'

Percy Grainger was once asked if he would consider conducting for Sir Thomas Beecham. He answered: 'Conduct for Sir Thomas Beecham? Certainly not! He has brown eyes.'

'a single man, Sir Thomas Beecham, did more for British music than was done by the massed battalions of the BBC. He was not only the greatest British conductor, he was also the greatest impresario of the age, endlessly stimulating and naturally disliked by everyone except his appreciative audiences.'

A.J.P. Taylor *English History 1914–1945* (1965)

'I was the most ordinary and, in some ways, the most satisfactory kind of youngster any parents could wish to have. I disliked noise of any sort, never indulged in it myself, was a model of taciturnity and gentle melancholy, and altogether an embryonic hero for a Bulwer-Lytton novel.'

Thomas Beecham *A Mingled Chime* (1944)

Beethoven, Ludwig van
(1770–1827)

'Keep your eye on him. He'll make the world talk some day.'

Wolfgang Amadeus Mozart

'Beethoven is a monster. With no respect for the nature of instruments. Clarity and precision are meaningless to him.'

Carl Maria von Weber

'Beethoven always sounds to me like the upsetting of a bag of nails, with here and there an also dropped hammer.'

John Ruskin, in a letter to John Brown, 6 Feb 1881

'His music always reminds one of paintings of battles.'

Bertolt Brecht, quoted in **Hubert Witt** *Brecht as they Knew him* (1974)

'... unanimous admiration has never been granted to Rameau, Bach, Mozart, Schubert, Wagner, Debussy and many other composers who have endowed music with discoveries more fertile or more original or positive than Beethoven; however, this unanimity has sprung to life quite effortlessly round his name. For some years now, important musicians have shown signs of surprise at this anomaly, and hope that posterity will value with more precision and justice the contribution of a great musician whose character has been unwittingly misrepresented in literature. It is striking to realize that, in fact, Beethoven owes his dictatorship more to poets and novelists than to musicians.'

Emile Vuillermoz *Histoire de la musique* (1949)

'His build was thick-set, with big bones and strong muscles; his extra-large head was covered with long, unkempt, almost completely grey hair, giving him a somewhat savage appearance. His forehead was high and broad, his eyes small and brown, almost retreating into his head when he laughed.... When he smiled, a most benevolent and amiable look spread over his face, especially encouraging to strangers with whom he spoke. His laughter, on the other hand, often burst out immoderately, distorting the intelligent and strongly marked features; the huge head seemed to swell as the face became still broader, so that the whole effect was often that of a grimacing caricature.... His eyes could suddenly grow unnaturally large and prominent, rolling and flashing, their pupils usually turned upward – or quite motionless, staring fixedly ahead when some idea seized him. When that happened, his whole appearance would be changed, with such an obviously inspired and impressive look that his small figure would seem to measure up to his mighty spirit. These moments of sudden inspiration often came over him, even in the jolliest company, and also in the street, attracting the notice of passers-by. Only his gleaming eyes and his face showed what was going on inside him....'

Anton F. Schindler *Beethoven as I knew him* (1840), edited by D. MacArdle (1966)

By the summer of 1802 Beethoven was deeply depressed, largely because he realized he was probably incurably deaf. He went to the healing baths in the village of Heiligenstadt, near Vienna (it is now a suburb of the city). There he wrote a document now known as the 'Heiligenstadt Testament', a kind of will addressed to his brothers Carl and Johann. It is dated 6 October at the beginning and 10 October at its conclusion.

'... just think, for the last six years I have been afflicted with an incurable complaint which has been made worse by incompetent doctors. From year to year my hopes of being cured have gradually been shattered, and finally I have been forced to accept the prospect of a permanent infirmity.... Though fond of the distractions offered by society I was soon obliged to seclude myself and live in solitude.... If I appear in company I am overcome by a burning anxiety, a fear that I am running the risk of letting people know of my condition. How humiliated I have felt if someone standing beside me heard the sound of a flute in the distance and I heard nothing, or if somebody heard a shepherd sing and again I heard nothing. Such experiences almost made me despair, and I was on the point of putting an end to my life. The only thing that held me back was my art. For indeed it seemed impossible to leave this world before I had produced all the works that I felt the urge to compose; and thus I have dragged on this miserable existence.... Almighty God who look down into my innermost soul, you see into my heart and you know that it is filled with love for humanity and a desire to do good. Oh, my fellow men, when some day you read this statement, remember that you have done me wrong.... I herewith nominate you both heirs to my small property.... Divide it honestly, live in harmony and help one another. Well, that is all. Joyfully I go to meet death – should it come before I have had an opportunity of developing my artistic gifts, then in spite of my hard fate it would still come too soon.... Farewell, and when I am dead do not wholly forget me.'

Quoted in **R.M. James** *Beethoven* (1983)

'It is to be feared, should Beethoven pursue this road in his music, that his public will leave the concert hall with uneasy feelings. This will be the result of the unaccustomed complexity of the musical ideas, and the ceaseless blowing of all instruments simultaneously.'

Viennese music correspondent, writing after the first performance of Beethoven's Symphony no.3 in E flat at the Theater an der Wien on 7 April 1805

'*The Rage over a Lost Penny* is a rondo by Beethoven. What could be merrier than this jest? In spite of myself, I laughed from beginning to end while playing it over for the first time. It is the most harmless, amiable rage such as one feels when one can't get one's shoe off; one perspires and stamps one's foot while the shoe looks up phlegmatically at its owner. Now I have you, Beethovenians, who swoon and turn up the whites of your eyes as you cry in exaltation: "Beethoven always sought the sublime, and freed from earthly cares, he flew from star to star!" His favourite expression when he felt in a good mood was: "Today I feel altogether unbuttoned!" And then he would laugh like a lion and beat about him – untamable in that as in everything.'

Robert Schumann, in the *Neue Zeitschrift für Musik* (1840)

'The grandeur of Beethoven's thirty-second piano sonata (in C minor, op.111) represents the opening of the gates of heaven.'

Robert Browning, quoted in **Donald Thomas**: *Robert Browning – a Life Within Life* (1982)

'From the heart – may it go back – to the heart.' ['Von Herzen – möge es wieder – zu Herzen gehn']

Beethoven's inscription on the manuscript of his *Missa solemnis*, completed in 1823

In 1860 Richard Wagner was in Paris for the production of his *Tannhäuser*. Rossini was living in Paris at this time. He had retired from composing operas since writing *William Tell* in 1829. He was sixty-eight years old, Wagner was forty-seven. They met at Rossini's house and enjoyed an amicable conversation. Among the matters they discussed were the works of Beethoven. Rossini had heard some Beethoven quartets in Milan as a young man and had been very impressed. He told Wagner that he had then heard the *Eroica* Symphony in Vienna, and was 'completely knocked over'. This made him determined to meet this great musical genius somehow. He had a contact through the Italian poet Carpani. Beethoven told Carpani that he was agreeable that Rossini should visit him. Rossini was in Vienna in 1822 for the production of his opera *Zelmira*. He told Wagner that the portraits of Beethoven give a very vivid impression of what he looked like but no painting could fully realize the indefinable sadness of his features. His voice was soft and rather veiled. As they entered the room Beethoven was correcting some proofs. He suddenly looked up and said in quite good Italian: 'Ah! Rossini – so you're the composer of *The Barber of Seville*. I congratulate you. It is an excellent *opera buffa* which I have read with great pleasure. It will be played as long as Italian opera exists. . . .' Rossini then expressed his deepest admiration for Beethoven's genius and his gratitude for having been allowed to visit him in person and to voice his sense of gratitude. Beethoven sighed and said: 'O un infelice!' ('Oh! Unhappy me!'). Rossini told Wagner that Beethoven's lodgings were so dingy and delapidated, and Beethoven was so personally isolated and destitute, that as he left he could not help weeping. That evening Rossini attended a banquet at Prince Metternich's mansion:

'Conscious of a feeling almost of resentment against the consideration shown to himself by the brilliant society of Vienna, he tried to persuade several of the people he met to subscribe towards a permanent income for Beethoven. Nobody, however, would have anything to do with the scheme, assuring him that, even if Beethoven were provided with a house, he would very soon sell it, for it was his habit to change his abode every six months and his servants every six weeks. . . . Among the music performed was one of Beethoven's trios, rapturously applauded. The contrast between the squalor in which the composer lived and elegance of the surroundings . . . again struck Rossini with a sense of tragic incongruity.'

Francis Toye *Rossini: a Study in Tragi-Comedy* (1934)

Bellini, Vincenzo (1801–35)

'Signor Bellini is a very young composer, whose labours are supposed to have received the help of more experienced hands in the construction of this opera.... As a musical composition the opera is not destitute of merit, with the exception of the overture, which is very weak and puerile. It is deficient in concerted pieces, because the incidents of the drama hardly afford situations which call for any: but a pleasing vein of melody prevails throughout the whole.'

From a review of *Il Pirata*, the first Bellini opera heard in London, in *The Times* (18 April 1830)

'We cannot ... award any high praise to this opera of Bellini's. It is lamentably deficient in original ideas (Rossini, as usual, being the source principally drawn upon) and but for a certain dramatic character discernible in its music would, unusually short as it is, put the patience of the audience to a somewhat severe test.'

From a review of *Norma*, in *The Morning Post* (24 June 1833)

'Comparisons and contrasts among Rossini, Bellini, and Donizetti always are interesting, and can be used as valuable tools of insight and criticism. It is clear, for example, that Donizetti to the end of his active life remained what Rossini had been until after the composition of *Semiramide* in 1822–23 – an artisan whose métier was the provision of operas as fast as he could compose them and impresarios would stage them – whereas Bellini, almost from the beginning, had been something very different, a precursor of the Romantic composers of opera to whom each new work was to be a very carefully elaborated unique creative effort. But trying to decide which of the three composers was "greater" than the other two is bootless: Bellini would have been as incapable of the abounding wit of *Il Barbiere di Siviglia* or *Don Pasquale*, the massiveness of *Guillaume Tell*, or the Verdian passion of *Anna Bolena* as Rossini would have been of composing *Norma* or Donizetti *La Sonnambula*. But there can be no doubt that Rossini was the most versatile and roundly human of the three men, as Donizetti was the most kindly and humane.'

Herbert Weinstock *Donizetti and the World of Italian Opera in Italy, Paris, and Vienna in the First Half of the Nineteenth Century* (1963)

'In the two periods before and after the 1939–45 war, *Norma* acquired two great protagonists: Rosa Ponselle and Maria Callas.... With such exponents, *Norma*, above all Bellini's operas, flowers, gains in expressiveness and dramatic impact and the music grows to full stature as it cannot when the performance is in lesser hands. Partly, this gain is general and the result of technical attainments, of superior, more penetrating imagination; partly it is particular and the product of an ability to colour and weight every phrase individually and leave nothing open to the risks of the automatic or the routine. But, whatever the reason, let no one imagine he has genuinely heard *Norma* without a truly great singer in the title role. Not to have one is as dire in its consequences as a performance of *Götterdämmerung* with an inadequate Brünnhilde. The trouble as far as Bellini is concerned is that, in the twentieth century, there have been fewer great Normas than fine Brünnhildes.'

George Henry Hubert Lascelles, 7th Earl of Harewood, in *Kobbé's Complete Opera Book* (9th edition 1979)

'No gentleman can fail to admire Bellini.'

W.H. Auden

Benedict, Sir Julius (1804–85)

Benedict's *The Lily of Killarney*, based on Dion Boucicault's celebrated melodrama, *Colleen Bawn*, was one of the most successful British operas of Victorian times. Boucicault did not have much faith in opera and opera composers and he went to the rehearsals with some misgivings, very concerned at the way in which his lamb might be butchered into marketable form for operatic consumption. He published an account of his reactions on seeing the opera, to which he went with its librettist John Oxenford:

'All the sentiment, all the tenderness, all the simple poetry was swept away. . . . I could have cried over it, but it was so drolly burlesque that as I sat and witnessed the attempted murder of Eily, laughter got the best of us both: "Yes", said John, "But listen to that!" The house was on its feet, and amid enthusiastic shouts the singers were called out to receive an ovation.'

Dion Boucicault Opera, in *North American Review* (April 1887)

Berg, Alban (1885–1935)

The Royal College of Music rejected Benjamin Britten's suggestion that the college library should have the score of Schoenberg's *Pierrot lunaire*. While he was in his last year there as a student in 1933 he hoped to use funds from a scholarship he had won to study in Vienna with Berg:

'When College was told coolness arose. I think, but I can't be sure, that the Director [Sir Hugh Allen] put a spoke in the wheel. At any rate, when I said at home during the holidays: "I *am* going to study with Berg,

aren't I?'' the answer was a firm: ''No, dear''. Pressed,
my mother said: ''He's not a good influence. . . .'''

Benjamin Britten, in Britten Looking Back, in *The Sunday Telegraph* (17 Nov 1963)

Berlioz, Hector (1803–69)

King of Prussia: 'I understand that you are the composer
who writes for five hundred musicians?'

Hector Berlioz: 'Your Majesty has been misinformed. I
sometimes write for four hundred and fifty.'

Quoted in *Grove's Dictionary of Music and Musicians* 5th
edition (1954)

'Berlioz is France's greatest composer, alas. A musician
of great genius, and little talent.'

Maurice Ravel

'His orchestration is so dirty that I have to wash my
hands after turning over the pages of his scores.'

Felix Mendelssohn, in a verbal comment to Schumann

'There is much in his music that is insufferable, but also a
lot that is extremely intelligent and even full of genius.
Sometimes he produces the effect on me of the helpless
King Lear in person.'

Robert Schumann

'The ordinary orchestra, the ordinary chorus, the ordinary concert-room would never do for him; everything
must be magnified . . . beyond life-size. Similarly in his
prose, the ordinary similes, the ordinary metaphors
rarely occur to him; the dilated brain can only express
itself in a dilation of language . . . one adjective is rarely
enough for Berlioz; there must generally be at least three,
and these of the most exaggerated kind. A thing is never
beautiful or ugly for Berlioz; it is either divine or
horrible.'

Ernest Newman *Berlioz: Romantic and Classic*, edited by
Peter Heyworth (1972)

Bernstein, Leonard (born 1918)

'Lenny is a short, trim man, and yet he always seems tall.
It is his head. He has a noble head, with a face that is at
once sensitive and rugged, and a full stand of iron-gray
hair, with sideburns. . . . His success radiates from his
eyes and his smile with a charm that illustrates Lord
Jersey's adage that ''contrary to what the Methodists tell
us, money and success are good for the soul''. Lenny

may be fifty one, but he is still the *Wunderkind* of American music.... He is the man who more than any other has broken down the wall between elite music and popular tastes....'

Tom Wolfe, in 'Radical Chic & Mau-Mauing the Flak Catchers', *The New Journalism*, edited by **Tom Wolfe** and **E.W. Johnson** (1975)

Bismarck, Otto von (1815–98)

Tsar Alexander III visited Berlin in 1889 and Bismarck left his retirement in the country to meet him. When the tsar went to the opera, Bismarck accompanied him:

'It was his only appearance there since he became Chancellor. He saw *Rheingold*, but made no comment; it cannot have been much to his taste, which stopped with Chopin.'

A.J.P. Taylor *Bismarck: the Man and the Statesman* (1955)

Bizet, Georges (1838–75)

'out of such material it was not difficult to construct an operatic plot. The chief wonder is that Verdi did not get hold of it before Bizet. If he had, we should certainly have been richer by another opera with a distressing end to a career of questionable conduct in the chief characters ... the gipsy melodies impart a flavour, if it may be so termed, to the opera – a flavour of musical garlic so to speak, which gives a special piquancy to the whole, and yet does not destroy the characteristic quality of the other materials.'

From a review of *Carmen* in *The Whitehall Review* (22 June 1878)

'Yesterday evening – to rest from my own work – I played through Bizet's *Carmen* from cover to cover. I consider it a *chef-d'oeuvre* in the fullest sense ... one of those rare compositions which seem to reflect most strongly the musical tendencies of a whole generation. It seems to me that our period differs from earlier ones in this one characteristic: contemporary composers *are engaged in the pursuit of charming and piquant effects*, unlike Mozart, Beethoven, Schubert and Schumann ... contemporary music is clever, piquant, and eccentric, but cold and lacking the glow of true emotion. And behold, a Frenchman comes on the scene, in whom these qualities of piquancy and pungency are not the outcome of effort and reflection, but flow from his pen as in a free stream, flattering the ear, but touching it also.... I cannot play the last scene without tears in my eyes; the gross rejoicings of the crowd who look on at the bullfight, side by side with this, the poignant tragedy and death of the two principal characters. . . .'

Pyotr Il'yich Tchaikovsky, in a letter to Madame von Meck, July 1880

Bloch, Ernest (1880–1962)

'In certain epochs of history, broad truths, social, political or religious, have set up wide currents of thought and feeling that have swept man along in a unity of action and of faith. In such time, art has been one with life and its expression has stood for humanity. Egypt, Greece, the Middle Ages, the Renaissance knew such an art. It seems to me that the latest example of one of these collective states of soul in music was Richard Wagner; for in him we find incarnate the future dream and development of his race. But since Wagner's time no great conception, no great conviction has fertilized mankind. On the other hand, the critical instinct has developed, the positive sciences have reigned; industrialism and the vulgarization of art, heightened communication and interchange of ideas have foisted on our consciousness a febrile mixture of thought and feeling. We find the most hostile theories living side by side. The old convictions are shattered, and new ideas are not strong enough to become convictions. Everywhere there is chaos. And art indeed has been the mirror of our uncertainties. It is significant to find, in a single epoch, the flourishing of works and styles so varied and so opposed: Reger to Strauss, Mahler to Schoenberg; Saint-Saens to d'Indy or Debussy; Puccini to Dukas. Our arts tend more and more toward an individualistic, non-representative and non-racial expression. Nor is the factitious renaissance of national arts which manifested itself before the war to be taken seriously. The ardour of these prophets was an affair of the will, of the intellect. Their influence on the real domain of art is negligible.

There can be no doubt . . . that a great artist like Claude Debussy stands for the best and purist traditions of the French. But he is representative chiefly aesthetically and in form. The essence of his inspiration has little in common with the present state of France. He stands far less for France than a Rabelais, a Montaigne, a Voltaire, a Balzac, a Flaubert. He represents in reality only a small part of his country.'

Ernest Bloch *Man and Music* (1916)

Boieldieu, François Adrien (1775–1834)

Boieldieu's opera *Le calife de Bagdad*, first performed at the Opéra Comique in Paris in September 1800, was one of the great successes of the age and one of the landmarks of the European fascination with the exotic qualities of the Middle East, then much in vogue. After a performance in Paris Cherubini is said to have remarked to Boieldieu: 'Aren't you ashamed of such undeserved success?'

Bold, Alan (born 1943)

RECITATIVE

(to Ronald Stevenson)

'Come, let's away to prison;
We two alone will sing like birds in the cage.'
— SHAKESPEARE, *King Lear*

'Whereas a man may have noon audience,
Noght helpeth it to tellen his sentence.'
— CHAUCER, *Prologue to the Nun's Priest's Tale*

You ask a poet to sing
Why
Even the birds are hoarse.
The nightingale that long ago
Numbed Keats, is dead.
What of the wind whispering through the trees
When no one cares to hear?
Perhaps you think –
'Ah! the golden skinned lassies
Can still move a poet.'

Once I sang
But that was before I knew
What went on in the world.
Yes! I was blithe,
Chirping away happily,
And, like Chauntecleer, closing my eyes
To do it.
I was, however, ignoring
The modern world
With all its blessings
And all its faults.
When I saw gestant China
Bear well – I rejoiced,
But did not sing.
Could I ignore the toll of the struggle?

Damn it!
Our voices are not made for singing now
But for straight-talking.
As the sea-surge turns over more filth
We may do some good
By exposure.
Look at the moon tonight

Or at the sea.
But before an easy praise of nature
Reflect on those folk
Who have not our sensitive thoughts,
For whom bread, not words, is life:
They matter.

Song implies melody; but the poet
Is after harmony.
Speaking for myself.
Songs have been sung
And dances have been danced
And slaves have done the singing
And peasants have done the dancing
To lessen their hell.
It may be that after this
When people are really allowed
To live,
The birds will sing afresh,
And then the poets will join them.
But for the present
We have enough songs that lie
Unsung.
Most of them by great singers.
Our job is to try
To change things.
After Hiroshima
You ask a poet to sing.

Alan Bold *In This Corner* (1983)

Boult, Sir Adrian (1889–1982)

'Never try to tell a man how to play his instrument: he knows far more about it than you do, and will immediately resent your effort. Instead, explain exactly what it is you want, and leave it to him to produce the desired tone, effect, or whatever it is.'

Quoted in **Donald Brook** *Conductors' Gallery* (1947)

Brahms, Johannes (1833–97)

'This month introduced us to a wonderful person, Brahms, a composer from Hamburg, twenty years old. Here again is one of those who come straight from the hand of God. He played us sonatas, scherzos etc. of his own, all of them showing exuberant imagination, depth and feeling, and mastery of form. Robert says that there was nothing that he could tell him to take away or to add.

   It is really moving to see him sitting at the piano, with his interesting young face, which becomes transfigured when he plays, his beautiful hands, which over come the greatest difficulties with perfect ease ... what he played to us is so masterly that one cannot but think that the good God sent him into the world ready-made. He has a great future before him. ... '

Clara Schumann's diary entry after meeting Brahms on 30 Sept 1853; quoted in **Irving Kolodin** *The Composer as Listener* (1958)

In 1862 Brahms paid his first visit to Vienna, which was to become his second home. Eduard Hanslick recounts his first concert:

'It may appear praiseworthy to Brahms that he plays more like a composer than a virtuoso, but such praise is not altogether unqualified. Prompted by the desire to let the composer speak for himself, he neglects – especially in the playing of his own pieces – much that the player should rightly do for the composer. His playing resembles the austere Cordelia, who concealed her finest feelings rather than betray them to the people. The forceful and the distorted are thus simply impossible in Brahms's playing. Its judicious softness is, indeed, such that he seems reluctant to draw a full tone from the piano. As little as I wish to gloss over the minor shortcomings, just as little do I wish to deny how insignificant they are compared with the irresistible spiritual charm of his playing.'

Eduard Hanslick *Music Criticisms 1846–99*, translated and edited by **Henry Pleasants** (1951)

'I played over the music of that scoundrel Brahms. What a giftless bastard!'

Pyotr Il'yich Tchaikovsky, in his diary, entry for 9 Oct 1886

'There are some sacrifices which should not be demanded twice from any man, and one of them is listening to Brahms' *Requiem*.'

George Bernard Shaw, in a review in *The Star*; quoted in **Hesketh Pearson** *Bernard Shaw: his Life and Personality* (1942)

'Brahms's northern heritage deeply pervades his music. It is the sea that surges through all his harmonies – the northern sea with its long, heavy breakers.'

Emil Ludwig *The Germans* (1942)

Brahms was once present in the concert hall in Leipzig while Arthur Nikisch was rehearsing one of the composer's symphonies. Brahms could hardly get over his surprise at what he was hearing the orchestra play, although it was his own music. Nikisch recorded that Brahms became quite nervous and that he kept repeating: 'Is it possible? Did I really write that?' But after the rehearsal, Brahms said to Nikisch: 'You have changed everything. But you are right – it *must* be like that', and he was beaming all over his face.

Quoted in **David Wooldridge** *Conductor's World* (1970)

'Bogus greatness, long drawn out.'

Darius Milhaud (born 1892)

BBC

'Music has a very great deal for which to thank the BBC, which has taught the uncultured public that a symphony is not so deadly as hyoscyamine, nor as painful as mumps.'

Ernest Irving, quoted in **Donald Brook** *Conductors' Gallery* (1947)

Britten, Benjamin (1913–76)

At the age of 22 Britten was contracted to write the score for a documentary film, *Coal Face*, devised and directed by Alberto Cavalcanti. This came about after a letter was sent to the Royal College of Music, asking if they had 'a bright young student who could write a little incidental music. . . .'

Benjamin Britten, in a letter to Paul Rotha, 15th July 1970; quoted in **Charles Osborne** *W.H. Auden: the Life of a Poet* (1979)

'One had always been told that English was impossible to set or to sing. Since I already knew the songs of the Elizabethan composers . . . I knew this to be false, but the influence of that great composer, Handel, on the setting of English had been unfortunate. . . . Here at last was a composer who could both set the language . . . and at the same time write music to which it was a real pleasure to listen.'

W.H. Auden, in an unpublished tribute to Britten on his 50th birthday; quoted in **Donald Mitchell** *Britten and Auden in the Thirties* (1981)

'There are many dangers that hedge round the unfortunate composer: pressure groups that demand true proletarian music, snobs who demand the latest avant-garde tricks; critics who are already trying to document today for tomorrow, to be the first to find the correct pigeonhole definition. These people are dangerous . . . because they may make the composer, above all the young composer, self-conscious, and instead of writing his own music, music that springs naturally from his gift and personality, he may be frightened into writing pretentious nonsense, or deliberate obscurity. He may find himself writing more and more for machines, in conditions dictated by machines, and not by humanity; or, of course, he may end by creating grandiose claptrap when his real talent is for dance tunes or children's piano pieces. Finding one's place in society as a composer is not a straightforward job. It is not helped by the attitude toward the composer of some societies. . . .

The *ideal* conditions for an artist or musician will never be found outside the *ideal* society, and when shall we see that? But I think I can tell you some of the things that any artist demands from any society. He demands that his art shall be accepted as an essential part of human activity and human expression; and that he shall be accepted as a genuine practitioner of that art and consequently of value to the community; reasonably, he demands a secure living from society, and a pension when he has worked long enough. . . .'

Benjamin Britten, writing in the *Saturday Review* (22 August 1964)

Browning, Robert (1812–89)

I.

Oh Galuppi, Baldassaro, this is very sad to find!

I can hardly misconceive you; it would prove me deaf
and blind;

But although I take your meaning, 'tis with such a heavy
mind!

II.

Here you come with your old music, and here's all the
good it brings.

What, they lived once thus at Venice where the
merchants were the kings,

Where Saint Mark's is, where the Doges used to wed the
sea with rings?

III.

Ay, because the sea's the street there; and 'tis arched by
. . . what you call

. . . Shylock's bridge with houses on it, where they kept
the carnival:

I was never out of England – it's as if I saw it all.

IV.

Did young people take their pleasure when the sea was
warm in May?

Balls and masks begun at midnight, burning ever
to mid-day,

When they made up fresh adventures for the morrow,
do you say?

V.

Was a lady such a lady, cheeks so round and lips
so red, –

On her neck the small lace buoyant, like a bell-flower on
    its bed,
O'er the breast's superb abundance where a man might
    base his head?

VI.

Well, and it was graceful of them – they'd break talk off
    and afford
– She, to bite her mask's black velvet – he, to finger on
    his sword,
While you sat and played Toccatas, stately at
    the clavichord?

VII.

What? Those lesser thirds so plaintive, sixths
    diminished, sigh on sigh,
Told them something? Those suspensions, those
    solutions – 'Must we die?'
Those commiserating sevenths – 'Life might last! we can
    but try!'

VIII.

'Were you happy?' – 'Yes.' – 'And are you still as happy?'
    'Yes. And you?'
– 'Then, more kisses!' – 'Did *I* stop them, when a million
    seemed so few?'
Hark, the dominant's persistence till it must be
    answered to!

IX.

So, an octave struck the answer. Oh, they praised you, I
    dare say!
'Brave Galuppi! that was music! good alike at grave
    and gay!
I can always leave off talking when I hear a
    master play!'

X.

Then they left you for their pleasure: till in due time, one
    by one,
Some with lives that came to nothing, some with deeds
    as well undone,
Death stepped tacitly and took them where they never
    see the sun.

XI.

But when I sit down to reason, think to take my stand
    nor swerve,
While I triumph o'er a secret wrung from nature's
    close reserve,
In you come with your cold music till I creep through
    every nerve.

XII.

Yes, you, like a ghostly cricket, creaking where a house
    was burned:
'Dust and ashes, dead and done with, Venice spent what
    Venice earned.
The soul, doubtless, is immortal – where a soul can
    be discerned.'

XIII.

'Yours for instance: you know physics, something
    of geology,

Mathematics are your pastime; souls shall rise in
their degree;
Butterflies may dread extinction, – you'll not die, it
cannot be!'
XIV.
'As for Venice and her people, merely born to bloom
and drop,
Here on earth they bore their fruitage, mirth and folly
were the crop:
What of soul was left, I wonder, when the kissing had
to stop?'
XV.
'Dust and ashes!' So you creak it, and I want the heart
to scold.
Dear dead women, with such hair, too – what's become
of all the gold
Used to hang and brush their bosoms? I feel chilly and
grown old.

Robert Browning *A Toccata of Galuppi's* (1847)
(Baldassare Galuppi (1706–85) was a composer and
organist at St. Mark's, Venice, famous for his light operas.)

Abt Vogler
(after he has been extemporizing upon the musical
instrument of his invention.)
I.
Would that the structure brave, the manifold music
I build,
Bidding my organ obey, calling its keys to their work,
Claiming each slave of the sound, at a touch, as when
Solomon willed
Armies of angels that soar, legions of demons
that lurk,
Man, brute, reptile, fly, – alien of end and of aim,
Adverse, each from the other heaven-high,
hell-deep removed, –
Should rush into sight at once as he named the
ineffable Name,
And pile him a palace straight, to pleasure the princess
he loved!
II.
Would it might tarry like this, the beautiful building
of mine,
This which my keys in a crowd pressed and
importuned to raise!
Ah, one and all, how they helped, would dispart now
and now combine,
Zealous to hasten the work, heighten their master
his praise!
And one would bury his brow with a blind plunge down
to hell,
Burrow awhile and build, broad on the roots of things,
Then up again swim into sight, having based me my
palace well,
Founded it, fearless of flame, flat on the
nether springs.

III.

And another would mount and march, like the excellent
minion he was,
    Ay, another and yet another, one crowd but with
    many a crest,
Raising my rampired walls of gold as transparent
    as glass,
    Eager to do and die, yield each his place to the rest:
For higher still and higher (as a runner tips with fire,
    When a great illumination surprises a festal night –
Outlining round and round Rome's dome from space
    to spire)
    Up, the pinnacled glory reached, and the pride of my
    soul was in sight.

IV.

In sight? Not half! for it seemed, it was certain, to match
    man's birth,
    Nature in turn conceived, obeying an impulse as I;
And the emulous heaven yearned down, made effort to
    reach the earth,
    As the earth had done her best, in my passion, to scale
    the sky:
Novel splendours burst forth, grew familiar and dwelt
    with mine,
    Not a point nor peak but found and fixed its
    wandering star;
Meteor-moons, balls of blaze: and they did not pale
    nor pine,
    For earth had attained to heaven, there was no more
    near nor far.

V.

Nay more; for there wanted not who walked in the glare
    and glow,
    Presences plain in the place; or, fresh from
    the Protoplast,
Furnished for ages to come, when a kindlier wind
    should blow,
    Lured now to begin and live, in a house to their liking
    at last;
Or else the wonderful Dead who have passed through
    the body and gone,
    But were back once more to breath in an old world
    worth their new:
What never had been, was now; what was, as it shall
    be anon;
    And what is, – shall I say, matched both? for I was
    made perfect too.

VI.

All through my keys that gave their sounds to a wish of
    my soul,
    All through my soul that praised as its wish flowed
    visibly forth,
All through music and me! For think, had I painted
    the whole,
    Why, there had it stood, to see, nor the process so
    wonder-worth:

Had I written the same, made verse – still, effect
    proceeds from cause,
  Ye know why the forms are fair, ye hear how the tale
    is told;
It is all triumphant art, but art in obedience to laws,
  Painter and poet are proud in the artist-list enrolled:
VII.
But here is the finger of God, a flash of the will that can,
  Existent behind all laws, that made them and, lo,
    they are!
And I know not if, save in this, such gift be allowed
    to man,
  That out of three sounds he frame, not a fourth sound,
    but a star.
Consider it well: each tone of our scale in itself
    is nought;
  It is everywhere in the world – loud, soft, and all
    is said:
Give it to me to use! I mix it with two in my thought:
  And, there! Ye have heard and seen: consider and bow
    the head!
VIII.
Well, it is gone at last, the palace of music I reared;
  Gone! and the good tears start, the praises that come
    too slow;
For one is assured at first, one scarce can say that
    he feared,
  That he even gave it a thought, the gone thing was
    to go.
Never to be again! But many more of the kind
  As good, nay, better perchance: is this your comfort
    to me?
To me, who must be saved because I cling with my mind
  To the same, same self, same love, same God: ay, what
    was, shall be.
IX.
Therefore to whom turn I but to thee, the
    ineffable Name?
  Builder and maker, thou, of houses not made
    with hands!
What, have fear of change from thee who art ever
    the same?
  Doubt that thy power can fill the heart that thy
    power expands?
There shall never be one lost good! What was, shall live
    as before;
  The evil is null, is nought, is silence implying sound;
What was good shall be good, with, for evil, so much
    good more;
  On the earth the broken arcs; in the heaven, a
    perfect round.
X.
All we have willed or hoped or dreamed of good
    shall exist;
  Not its semblance, but itself; no beauty, nor good,
    nor power

Whose voice has gone forth, but each survives for
    the melodist
    When eternity affirms the conception of an hour.
The high that proved too high, the heroic for earth
    too hard,
    The passion that left the ground to lose itself in
      the sky,
The music sent up to God by the lover and the bard;
    Enough that he heard it once: we shall hear it
      by-and-by.
XI.
And what is our failure here but a triumph's evidence
    For the the fulness of the days? Have we withered
      or agonized?
Why else was the pause prolonged but that singing
    might issue thence?
    Why rushed the discords in but that harmony should
      be prized?
Sorrow is hard to bear, and doubt is slow to clear,
    Each sufferer says his say, his scheme of the weal
      and woe:
But God has a few of us whom he whispers in the ear;
    The rest may reason and welcome: 'tis we
      musicians know.
XII.
Well, it is earth with me; silence resumes her reign:
    I will be patient and proud, and soberly acquiesce.
Give me the keys. I feel the common chord again,
    Sliding by semitones, till I sink to the minor, – yes,
And I blunt it into a ninth, and I stand on alien ground,
    Surveying awhile the heights I rolled from into
      the deep;
Which, hark, I have dared and done, for my resting place
    is found,
    The C Major of this life: so, now I will try to sleep.

                              1864.

Robert Browning *Abt Vogler* (1864). (George Joseph
Vogler (1749–1814), teacher of Weber and Meyerbeer, was
renowned as an extraordinary extemporizer upon the organ.
He was the inventor of the Orchestrion, a small portable
organ. It was said this instrument sounded superb when
he played it, but weak when played by others.)

Bugle

Now deeper roll the maddening drums,
And the mingling host like ocean heaves;
While from the midst a horrid wailing comes,
And high above the fight the lonely bugle grieves.

Grenville Mellen 'Ode on the Celebration of the Battle of
Bunker Hill' (1825)

Our echoes roll from soul to soul,
And grow for ever and for ever.

Blow, bugle, blow, set the wild echoes flying,
And answer, echoes, answer, dying, dying, dying.

Alfred, Lord Tennyson *The Princess* (1847)

Blow out, you bugles, over the rich Dead!
There's none of these so lonely and poor of old,
But, dying, has made us rarer gifts than gold.
These laid the world away: gave up the years to be
Of work and joy, and that unhoped serene
That men call age, and those who would have been
Their sons, they gave their immortality.

Rupert Brooke 'The Dead' (1914)

Bruckner, Anton (1824–96)

'I know of only one who reaches up to Beethoven, and
that is Bruckner.'

Richard Wagner

Busoni, Ferruccio (1866–1924)

'Come, follow me into the realm of music. Here is the
iron fence which separates the earthly from the eternal.
Have you undone the fetters and thrown them away?
Now come. It is not as it was before when we stepped
into a strange country; we soon learnt to know everything there and nothing surprised us any longer. Here
there is no end to the astonishment, and yet from the
beginning we feel it is homelike.

You still hear nothing, because everything *sounds*.
Now already you begin to differentiate. Listen, every star
has its rhythm and every world its measure. And on each
of the stars and each of the worlds, the heart of every
separate living being is beating in its own individual
way. And all the beats agree and are separate and yet are
a whole.

Your inner ear becomes sharper. Do you hear the
depths and the heights? They are as immeasurable as
space and endless as numbers.

Unthought-of scales extend like bands from one world
to another, *stationary* and yet *eternally in motion*. Every
tone is the centre of immeasurable circles. And now
sound is revealed to you!

Innumerable are its voices; compared with them the
murmuring of the harp is a din; the blare of a thousand
trombones a chirrup. All, all melodies heard before or
never heard, resound completely and simultaneously,
carry you, hang over you, or skim lightly past you – of
love and passion, of spring and of winter, of melancholy
and of hilarity, they are themselves the souls of millions
of beings in millions of epochs. If you focus your

attention on one of them you perceive how it is connected with all the others, how it is combined with all the rhythms, coloured by all kinds of sounds, accompanied by all harmonies, down to unfathomable depths and up to the vaulted roof of heaven.

Now you realise how planets and hearts are one, that nowhere can there be an end or an obstacle, that infinity lives in the spirit of all beings; that each being is illimitably great and illimitably small: the greatest expansion is like a point; and that light, sound, movement and power are identical, and each separate and all united, they are life.'

Ferruccio Busoni, in a letter to his wife, 3 March 1910; in *The Essence of Music*, translated by Rosamond Ley (1957)

see also MacDiarmid, Hugh

Callas, Maria (1923–77)

'The advertisements claim: "Callas *is* Carmen". *Au contraire messieurs*, Carmen *is* Callas, every note imprinted with her individual stamp. You may find it too intrusive but ignore it you cannot ... the tessitura of the part and the present timbre of Callas's voice now seem perfectly matched. She is entirely inside the musical portrait and never at odds with it. ... Hers is a Carmen to haunt you.'

Philip Hope-Wallace, in *Gramophone* (Feb 1964)

Cardus, Neville (1889–1975)

Neville Cardus, distinguished cricket columnist and music critic of the *Manchester Guardian* describes one of the staunch Liberal readers of the *Guardian*. A representative figure of the men who formed the basis of the paper's circulation, and absorbed every word of it each day:

'This Liberal I came to know was a gaunt hatchet-faced man who, after the 1914–1918 war, occupied each week a side corner seat not far from mine at the Hallé Concerts in a cheaper part of the hall. It was a time of ruin in the Lancashire mills, and every Thursday evening I would see this man come to his place, looking worn and worried; then when the music began, his eyes would close, and at the end of a composition they sometimes opened as though from shock; and he never applauded. One evening, he approached me in the interval and, with dignity but obvious nervousness, introduced himself and wished to shake hands with the *Guardian's* critic. ... He was in the mid-sixties and he carried that morning's *Guardian* in his hand. ... Later he asked me to give an address to the "Literary Society" of the town in

which he lived; he was the founder and the chairman. I
went there on a bitter night in winter. The mills were
black and vacant; some of them had no window-panes.
My audience was made up of men and women of all
ages, some in cloth caps and shawls, some in white
winged collars (the Elders), nearly all of them showing
signs that they were feeling the pinch. I talked about the
songs of Hugo Wolf, using gramophone records for
illustrations. I have never since spoken to an audience so
quick of apprehension, and so absorbed and moved at
times – and at others so palpably not to be taken in by
immoderate speech.

At the end of the lecture, my chairman asked me to his
home for supper; a house of stone, built ages ago. Soon
he would have to give it up. . . . He had worked his way
up from a half-timer to a mill-manager. . . . Now he was
in fallen circumstances; the house had to go; he would
put it all into auctioneers' hands, live in lodgings and
take up an agency. But he'd keep his old yellow-keyed
upright piano, a Collard and Collard; and if he couldn't
buy a subscriber's ticket to next year's "Hallé," he'd go
"in shilling places," where he'd begun, in times when
"Norman-Neruda played Mendelssohn violin concerto
like you never hear it played now, so fine and delicate
and so like sunshine on t' hillside over yon, when it
shines at all." There was no self-pity, no bitterness.
"Ah've had a good life," he said; "and Ah've got
something there" – tapping his head – "that they can
never take from me in a hurry." '

Neville Cardus *Second Innings* (1950)

Caruso, Enrico (1873–1921)

'Recordings had won him the affections of millions, who
sat by their phonographs and thrilled to the impassioned
arias. His countrymen wept in exile over nostalgic folk
songs winewarm with sunlight. . . . To New York's Little
Italy he was far more than a voice; he had become a
symbol of hope and laughter in adversity. They iden-
tified fiercely, patriotically, with the chubby little man
who had escaped from a Neapolitan slum to win story
book success on alien soil but still spoke broken English
and remained as Italian as macaroni.'

Stanley Jackson *Caruso* (1972)

Castiglione, Baldassar (1478–1529)

A member of an ancient aristocratic family, Castiglione
wrote a very influential Renaissance text, *Il libro de
cortegiano* ('The Book of the Courtier', 1528); it is a
dialogue discussing the qualities of the ideal courtier.

Among his desirable attributes should be a love of music and an ability to perform it:

'I would not our Courtier do as many do, that as soon as they come to any place, and also in the presence of the great men with whom they have no acquaintance at all, without much entreating set out themselves to show as much as they know, yea and many times that they know not, so that a man would ween they came purposely to show themselves for that, and that it is their principal profession. Therefore let our Courtier come to show his music as a thing to pass the time withall, and as he were enforced to do it, and not in the presence of noblemen, nor of any great multitude. And for all he be skillful and doth well understand it, yet will I have him to dissemble the study and pains that a man must needs take in all things that are well done. And let him make semblance that he esteemeth but little of himself that quality, but in doing it excellently well, make it much esteemed of other men.'

Baldassar Castiglione *The Book of the Courtier*, translated by Thomas Hoby (1561)

Castrato

'I heard the famous eunuch Cifaccio sing in the new Popish Chapel this afternoon; it was indeed very rare, and with great skill. He came over from Rome, esteemed one of the best voices in Italy. Much crowding – little devotion.'

'I heard the famous singer Cifaccio, esteemed the best in Europe. Indeed his holding out and delicateness in extending and loosing a note [*sic*] with incomparable softness and sweetness was admirable; for the rest, I found him a mere wanton, effeminate child, very coy, and proudly conceited to my apprehension. He touched the harpsichord to his voice rarely well. This was before a select number of particular persons whom Mr. Pepys invited to his house; and this was obtained by particular favour and much difficulty, the Signor much disdaining to show his talent to any but princes.'

John Evelyn, *Diary*, entries for 30 Jan and 19 April 1687

Cello

'The cello is like a beautiful woman who has not grown older, but younger with time, more slender, more supple, more graceful.'

Pablo Casals, in *Time* (29 April 1957)

Chaliapin, Feodor (1873–1938)

'Mr. Chaliapin, a basso of whose commanding gifts we have all heard, made his debut in this country and achieved, let us hasten to add, a striking success. His voice is of beautiful quality, and the artist's use of it is masterly; but over and above these recommendations Mr. Chaliapin possesses histrionic powers of a compelling order. His face, bearing, and manner in the part of the crime-haunted ruler were extraordinarily eloquent, as suggesting always a man obsessed by the memory of a hideous deed and torn by contrition. . . .'

Review of Musorgsky's *Boris Godunov*, in which Chaliapin took the title role, in *The Daily Telegraph* (25 June 1913)

Chamber Music

'People who attend chamber music concerts are like Englishmen who go to church when abroad.'

W.H. Auden, quoted in **Charles Osborne** *W.H. Auden: The Life of a Poet* (1979)

Cherubini, Luigi (1760–1842)

'Cherubini . . . was a fine composer in his own way; but if I ever come across him in the Elysian Fields I will watch his face as I tell him that the Berlioz he so despised gets a thousand performances today to his one, while of the young rebel's fellow students at the Conservatoire who did so well in the examination, not so much as the name of one of them is known to the ordinary music lover today.'

Ernest Newman, in *The Sunday Times* (7 March 1943)

Chopin, Fryderyk (1810–49)

'Hats off, gentlemen, here is a genius!'

Robert Schumann, in the *Allgemeine Musikalische Zeitung* (1831)

'The great composer strove in vain to get accustomed to the lonely life. . . . The oppressive scenery of Valldemosa and the austere appearance of the monastery, with its empty churches, deserted chapels, and romantic cemetery and cloisters, all of which seemed like the decor for some grand opera . . . were in too violent a contrast with Chopin's character. He was *par excellence* the man of the world, who dreamed nostalgically of the city-life he knew, with its parties and receptions. . . .'

... during those long winter evenings when the rain rattled monotonously on the tiled roofs and on the windows of the cell and the wind whistled through the empty cloisters, Chopin played over and revised his earlier compositions. ...'

Bartomeu Ferra *Chopin and George Sand in Majorca,* translated by **R.D.F. Pring-Mill** (1961)

Elizier Fournier describes an evening spent in the company of Chopin and George Sand at Nohant in July 1846. He played for hours on end until midnight, encompassing all moods from the gay and the lilting, to the tragic and the brilliantly witty:

'Never have I heard a talent such as his: prodigious in its simplicity, softness, kindness and wit. In this last genre he played us a takeoff on a Bellini opera which had us in stitches, such was the finesse of observation and the witty mocking of Bellini's musical style and habits. Then he played a prayer, for Poles in distress, which brought tears to our eyes; then an Etude on the sound of the tocsin which made us shiver; then a funeral march, so grave, sombre, and sorrowful that our hearts swelled, our chests contracted, and all one could hear in the silence were a few ill-contained sighs caused by an emotion too deep to be dominated. Emerging from this sorrowful inspiration and recalled to himself after a moment of rest by several notes sung by Madame Sand, he had us listen to the jolly airs of a dance called the *bourrée* which is common to this part of the country. ...'

Elizier Fournier in a letter, July 1846, quoted in **Curtis Gate** *George Sand – A Biography* (1975)

'The entire works of Chopin present a motley surface of ranting hyperbole and excruciating cacophony. ... There is an excuse at present for Chopin's delinquencies: he is entrammelled in the enthralling bonds of that arch-enchantress, George Sand, celebrated equally for the number and excellence of her romances and her lovers.'

Review in *Musical World* (28 Oct 1841)

Choral Music

'To White Hall; and there in the Boarded Gallery did hear the music with which the King is presented this night by Monsieur Grebus, the Master of his Music; both instrumental (I think twenty-four violins) and vocal: an English song upon Peace. But, God forgive me! I never was so little pleased with a concert of music in my life. The manner of setting of words and repeating them out of order, and that with a number of voices, makes me sick, the whole design of vocal music being lost by it. Here was a great press of people; but I did not see many pleased with it, only the instrumental music he had brought by practice to play very just.'

Samuel Pepys *Diary*, entry for 1 Oct 1667

'I heard *Judith*, an oratorio, performed.... Some parts of it were exceedingly fine; but there are two things in all modern music which I could never reconcile to common sense. One is singing the same words ten times over; the other, singing different words by different persons, at one and the same time. And this in the most solemn addresses to God, whether by way of prayer or of thanksgiving. This can never be defended by all the musicians in Europe, till reason is quite out of date....'

John Wesley *Journals*, entry for 29 Feb 1764

Church Music

'Whence hath the church so many Organs and Musical Instruments? To what purpose, I pray you, is that terrible blowing of Bellows, expressing rather the cracks of Thunder, than the sweetness of a voice? ... in the meantime, the common people standing by, trembling and astonished, admire the sounds of the Organs, the noise of the Cymbals and Musical Instruments, the harmony of the Pipes and Cornetts....'

Ailred of Rievaulx *Speculum caritatis*, 12th century

'They have so much of it in England that the monks attend to nothing else. A set of creatures who ought to be lamenting their sins fancy they can please God by gurgling in their throats. Boys are kept in the English Benedictine colleges solely and simply to sing hymns to the Virgin.'

Erasmus, after visiting England at Sir Thomas More's invitation

'... instead of the ancient, grave, and solemn wind music accompanying the organ, was introduced a concert of twenty-four violins between every pause, after the French fantastic light way, better suiting a tavern, or playhouse, than a church.' [after the accession of Charles II]

John Evelyn *Diary*, entry for 21 Dec 1662

'On Thursday morning I went to St. Paul's to see the Charity children assembled, and hear their singing. Berlioz says it is the finest thing he ever heard in England; and this opinion of his induced me to go. I was not disappointed – it is worth doing once, especially as we got out before the sermon.'

George Eliot, diary entry for 2 June 1852

Clarinet

'The clarinet, though appropriate to the expression of the most poetic ideas and sentiments, is really an epic instrument – the voice of heroic love.'

Hector Berlioz *Grand traité d'instrumentation et d'orchestration modernes* (1843)

'An instrument of torture operated by a person with cotton in his ears.'

'There are two instruments that are worse than a clarinet – two clarinets.'

Ambrose Bierce *The Devil's Dictionary* (1911)

Leopold Stokowski seldom resisted the temptation to touch up the orchestration of composer's scores. Charles O'Connell recounts an occasion when he added a gratuitous part for bass clarinet to Schubert's 'Unfinished' Symphony: 'It so happens . . . that the player of this instrument was quite a temperamental gentleman as well as a composer, and when he saw Stokowski's addition to Schubert's score, he was possessed by fury.' The situation was saved by the orchestra's manager, Howard Skinner, who persuaded the bass clarinet player to sit through the work pretending to play but actually making no sound. It seems Stokowski did not notice.

Abram Chasins *Leopold Stokowski: a Profile* (1979)

Class

'Mozart, Haydn, Vivaldi and Purcell are upper-class composers. Brahms, Mahler, Schubert and Beethoven are upper-middle. Tschiakovsky, Grieg and Mendelssohn are lower-middle. . . .

In a recent survey it was discovered that people who own their own houses prefer classical music, but people in council houses prefer pop. One suspects that the house-owners claimed to prefer classical music because they felt they ought to, because it seems more upper-classical than pop. After all the announcers do talk in "posh" voices on Radio Three while the disc jockeys on Radio One and Capital all sound like yobbos.

The Radio Three voice is not in fact upper-class at all, it is Marghanita Laski/Patricia Hughes sen-si-tive, which involves speaking very slowly and deliberately to eradicate any trace of a regional accent, with all the vowel sounds, particularly the 'o's emphasized: "vi-oh-lins", "pee-ar-*noes*", "Vivald-ee", "ball-*ay*". The pronunciation of foreign composers and musical terms is also far too good. . . .'

Jilly Cooper *Class* (1979)

Conductors and Conducting

'. . . how many are there who, fancying that they are able to conduct, innocently injure their best scores! Beethoven, it is said, more than once ruined the performance of his symphonies, which he would conduct even at the time when his deafness had become almost complete.

. . . The example of Beethoven leads me at once to say that, if the direction of an orchestra appears to me very difficult for a blind man, it is indisputably impossible for a deaf one, whatever may have been his technical talent before losing his sense of hearing. The orchestral conductor should *see* and *hear*; he should be *active* and *vigorous*, should know the *composition*, and the *nature* and *compass* of the instruments, should be able to *read the score*, and possess – besides the especial talent of which we shall presently endeavour to explain the constituent qualities – other almost indefinable gifts, without which an invisible link cannot establish itself between him and those whom he directs; the faculty of transmitting to them his feeling is denied him, and thence power, empire, and guiding influence completely fail him. He is then no longer a conductor, a director, but a simple beater of time – supposing that he knows how to beat it, and divide it, regularly.

The performers should feel that *he* feels, comprehends, and is moved. Then his emotion communicates itself to those whom he directs, his inward fire warms them, his electric glow animates them, his force of impulse excites them. He throws around him the vital irradiations of musical art.'

Hector Berlioz *Le chef d'orchestre: théorie de son art* (1856)

'[George] Risely used to annoy the members of the orchestra by an unpleasant habit of spitting, in his excitement over big *sforzato* chords. One morning I happened to drop in during one of his rehearsals and was amazed to see about half-a-dozen umbrellas go up in the orchestra. Risely was furious.

"Gentlemen, what is the meaning of this?" A voice: "Well, sir, the rain from your mouth on the *sforzatos* reaches us here, and we had to decide between mackintoshes and umbrellas." That cured Risely of the habit. . . .'

Sir Henry J. Wood *My Life of Music* (1938)

'Conductors must give unmistakable and suggestive signals to the orchestra – not choreography to the audience.'

George Szell, quoted in *Newsweek* (12 May 1963)

'Make all your performances a grand improvisation!'

Arthur Nikisch, to **Sir Henry Wood** (attrib)

'The conductor himself produces no music, but does so by means of others, whom he must lead by gestures, words, and the power of his personality, and the result depends on his ability to handle people. In this respect, too, innate talent is of decisive importance – a talent for asserting one's own personality – and it needs to be developed by constant endeavour and by making the most of daily experiences. He who has been born without authority and is lacking in the essential dynamics originating in the sphere of the will cannot gain a firm footing as a conductor, even if he possesses musical talent, ability or knowledge. He may reach a point at which he will be able to express himself with masterly skill on the piano or the violin, but he will never be successful in welding an orchestra or an operatic company into an instrument of his own. The result of his conducting will be more impersonal, insignificant, and ineffective than that of a musician of lesser ability who has the natural gift of authority.'

Bruno Walter *Theme and Variations: an Autobiography* (1946)

'In music, you get better with age. It's only at forty that you get taste. The years from sixty to seventy-five get you maturity. In all things where nerves play a major role, age helps. When I first did the *Meistersinger* I almost needed an ambulance to get me home. Now I can relax. I know that technically the music will happen and I can think inside it.'

Herbert von Karajan, in an interview with **Brian Moynahan**, in *The Sunday Times* (20 March 1983)

'Never look at the brass – it only encourages them . . . on the other hand, never let the horns and the woodwind get out of your sight: if you can hear them at all, they are too loud . . . if you think that the brass are not loud enough, reduce their dynamics by two degrees. . . .'

Richard Strauss (attrib)

Copland, Aaron (born 1900)

'You may be sitting in a room reading this book. Imagine one note struck upon the piano. Immediately that one note is enough to change the atmosphere of the room – proving that the sound element in music is a powerful and mysterious agent, which it would be foolish to deride or belittle.'

Aaron Copland *What to Listen for in Music* (1939)

'It is one of the curiosities of the critical creative mind that although it is very much alive to the component parts of the finished work it cannot know everything that the work may mean to others. There is an unconscious part in each work – an element of what André Gide called *le part de Dieu*. I have often felt familiar, and yet again unfamiliar, with a new work of mine as it was being rehearsed for the first time – as if both the players and I myself had to accustom ourselves to its strangeness. The late Paul Rosenfeld once wrote that he saw the steel frames of skyscrapers in my Piano Variations. I like to think that the characterization was apt, but I must confess that the notion of skyscrapers was not at all in my mind when I was composing the Variations. In similar fashion an English critic, Wilfred Mellors, has found in the final movement of my Piano Sonata "a quintessential musical expression of the idea of immobility". "The music runs down like a clock," Mellors writes, "and dissolves away into eternity." That is probably a very apt description also, although I would hardly have thought of it myself. Composers often tell you that they don't read criticisms of their works. As you see, I am an exception. I admit to a curiosity about the slightest clue as to the meaning of a piece of mine – a meaning, that is, other than the one I know I have put there.'

Aaron Copland *Music and the Imagination* (1952)

Cor Anglais

'. . . perhaps the instrument's soft and melancholy tone was thought to resemble the muted quality of English speech, which always amuses foreigners.'

James A. MacGillivray, in *Musical Instruments through the ages*, edited by Anthony Baines (1961)

Costa, Michael (1808–84)

Costa was born in Naples and trained as a composer and singer. His reputation as an orchestral reformer is based largely on his new seating arrangement for orchestral players on the concert platform, which produced an entirely new orchestral sonority. Costa's arrangement is still standard on modern concert platforms. It was a popular innovation:

'A greater triumph never prevailed. The oldest members of the [Philharmonic] Society frankly admitted, that never before in this country had the great symphonies and overtures been so marvellously executed; and the critics have one and all handsomely acknowledged the genius of Costa in the management of his forces. It is necessary to enquire into the secret of such an important result, and the first point to be considered is in the disposition of the orchestra . . . a complete revolution has been effected. The rapid and almost perpendicular rise of the old plan was long a matter of complaint – now, the elevation is reduced considerably; players with drums and trombones etc., are no longer perched up in the roof to drown the stringed instruments, which are in a valley, with a formidable array of double basses in front, effectively to stifle the melody of the first violins. Costa has got rid of such monstrosities; and studying the principles of acoustics, he has sought, and successfully, to blend the various tones.'

Illustrated London News (17 March 1846)

Critics

In 1860 Rossini gave Richard Wagner some advice about not taking any notice of music critics; he described how he went to Vienna in 1822 for the production of his opera *Zelmira* and how Weber wrote furious articles against him. His counsel was simple:

'... answer them with silence and indifference. It works better, I assure you, than anger and argument. Spite is everywhere. If you start bandying words or blows with that termagent, rest assured she'll have the last say.... Though you see me wearing a wig, I can assure you it wasn't those bumpkins who cost me a single hair of my head.'

Gioachino Rossini, translated by Geoffrey Skelton, in the programme of the Welsh National Opera production of *The Barber of Seville* (1981)

Cymbals

'Praise him upon the well-tuned cymbals: praise him upon the loud cymbals.
Let every thing that hath breath: praise the Lord.'

Psalms 149: 5

'Though I speak with the tongues of men and of angels, and have not charity, I am become as sounding brass, or a tinkling cymbal.'

1 Corinthians 5: 3

'A crowd is not company, and faces are but a gallery of pictures, and talk but a tinkling cymbal, where there is no love.'

Francis Bacon, 'Of Friendship', *Essays* (1597)

Czerny, Carl (1791–1857)

'However diligent the critic may be, it is quite impossible for him to catch up with Herr Czerny. If I had enemies and wanted to destroy them, I would condemn them to listen to nothing but music like this.'

Robert Schumann, on Czerny's 302nd work, in the *Neue Zeitschrift für Musik*

Debussy, Claude (1862–1918)

John Barbirolli was conducting a factory concert in Wigan and was startled by his audience's wild applause of Debussy's *L'après midi d'un faune*. This was their favourite piece, not the more popular *Mastersingers* overture or the *Eine kleine Nachtmusik*:

'Flinging down his baton in his dressing room when it was all over, he said to Laurence Turner, the leader of the orchestra: "I can't get over it . . . the way they reacted to the *Après midi*, which was hissed when it was first heard in Paris. . . . I see the age of miracles is not yet passed".'

Article in *Manchester Evening News*; quoted in **Charles Rigby** *John Barbirolli: a Biographical Sketch* (1948)

'We were all irritated by the paroxysm-like sounds we were making, and as is often the case with orchestras, we simply refused to take this work [*La mer*] seriously. One jocular fellow at one of the back stands concocted a small boat of music paper. With a slight push of the foot, it sailed on a wooden sea, from basses through the 'celli and violas, the length of the platform. This childish idea met with such success that there was soon a whole fleet of small ships made from all kinds of paper wending their hazardous ways through an ocean of legs, instruments and sound, as Neptune, conceived by Claude Debussy, thundered his way to the end. . . .'

Pierre Monteux, in **Doris Monteux** *It's All in the Music: the Life and Work of Pierre Monteux* (1965)

'. . . the outstanding first "modern" opera to appear in the 20th century was . . . *Pelléas et Melisande* (1902). . . . Yet it is a medieval tale full of pathos and mystery, in which the characters, lacking depth, are oppressed as if in a nightmare or hallucination. They are not "whole" people, but lost symbols of incomprehensible reality. The music, as with much of Debussy's impressionism, is passive, boneless, and in its lack of structural contour as mindless as the characters. It is the mindlessness created by a keen intelligence baffled by the conflicts of life.'

Sidney Finkelstein *How Music Expresses Ideas* (1970)

Delius, Frederick (1862–1934)

'I would never have dreamed that anyone but myself could write such good music.'

Richard Strauss

When Delius was to conduct the first performance of his *In a Summer Garden* at a Philharmonic Society of London concert in 1908, he was asked for some 'analytic' material for the programme notes. He replied:

'I do not much care for the analytical programmes as they are generally done, and for modern impressionistic music they are entirely useless. Besides, I wish the audience to concentrate their attention entirely on listening to the music and not to have their attention drawn away by musical examples. The title *In a Summer Garden* puts them into the atmosphere of my work – that is really all I desire.'

Quoted in **Robert Elkin** *Royal Philharmonic: the Annals of the Royal Philharmonic Society* (1947)

'Delius never seemed to know exactly what he wanted. A violinist once played a passage of his in three entirely different ways, asking the composer each time if that was what he meant. Each time came the reply: "Yes".'

Bernard Shore *The Orchestra Speaks* (1937)

'A provincial Debussy.'

A.J.P. Taylor *English History 1914–1945* (1965)

'Delius, in spite of his bewitching harmonic experiments (or is it because of them?), belongs mentally to the eighties.'

Ralph Vaughan Williams, in an essay on Gustav Holst in *Music and Letters* **1** (1920)

Discord

Melodious discord, heavenly tune harsh sounding,
Ear's deep-sweet music, and heart's
    deep-sore wounding.

William Shakespeare *Venus and Adonis* (1593)

Discords make the sweetest airs,
And curses are a sort of prayers.

Samuel Butler *Hudibras*, Part iii, canto 1 (1663–78)

I never heard
So musical a discord, such sweet thunder.

William Shakespeare *A Midsummer Night's Dream*, Act IV, scene i (1595)

So discord oft in music makes the sweeter lay.

Edmund Spenser *The Faerie Queene*, Book iii, canto 2 (1590)

Donizetti, Gaetano (1797–1848)

Of all the operas based on Sir Walter Scott's *Bride of Lammermoor*, Donizetti's *Lucia di Lammermoor* is the best known. It seems that Donizetti and his librettist Salvatore Cammarano perceived that:

'... the love story was the emotional core of the novel. They knew that this was conducive to good, effective opera as it had evolved in Italy in the 1830's.... No Scottish local colour is manifest in either text or music. For all the disparaging things that have been said about the way Scott's story and its characters turn out in the operatic rendition, the test of time has proven that Cammarano and Donizetti knew what they were about.'

Jerome Mitchell *The Walter Scott Operas* (1977)

'It was painful, from start to finish.'

Gaetano Donizetti, in a letter to a friend after the first performance of his opera *Maria Stuarda* at La Scala, Milan, on 30 Dec 1835

Drum

Let's march without the noise of threatening drum.

William Shakespeare *Richard II*, Act III, scene iii (1595)

At their chamber-door I'll beat the drum
Till it cry sleep to death.

William Shakespeare *King Lear*, Act II, scene iv (1605)

The double double double beat
Of the thundering drum
Cries: 'Hark! the foes come;
Charge, charge, 'tis too late to retreat.'

John Dryden *A Song for St. Cecilia's Day* (1687)

I hate the drum's discordant sound
Parading round and round and round:
To me it talks of ravaged plains,
And burning towns, and ruined swains,
And mangled limbs, and dying groans,
And widows' tears, and orphans' moans;
And all that miser's hand bestows
To fill the catalogue of human woes.

John Scott (1730–83) *Ode on Hearing the Drum*

A veteran of the Quebec campaign 1759, the Spanish wars in Havana 1762, operations in Gibraltar 1782 and Cape St. Vincent testifies to the intoxicating effects of the beating of the drum:

I am a son of Mars who has been in many wars,

And show my cuts and scars wherever I come;
This here was for a wench, and that other in a trench,
When welcoming the French at the sound of the drum.

Lal de laundle, etc.

My apprenticeship I past where my leader breathed
    his last
When the bloody die was cast on the heights of Abram;
And I served out my trade when the gallant game
    was play'd,
And the Moro low was laid at the sound of the drum.

I lastly was with Curtis among the floating batt'ries,
And there I left for witness an arm and a limb;
Yet let my country need me, with Elliott to head me,
I'd clatter on my stumps at the sound of a drum.

And now tho' I must beg, with a wooden arm and leg,
And many a tatter'd rag hanging over my bum,
I'm as happy with my wallet, my bottle and my callet,
As when I used in scarelet to follow the drum.

What tho', with hoary locks, I must stand the
    winter shocks,
Beneath the woods and rocks oftentimes for a home,
When tother bag I sell, and tother bottle tell,
I could meet a troop of hell, at the sound of a drum.

Robert Burns 'I am a Son of Mars', from *The Jolly Beggars:
A Cantata* (1785)

Ah, monarchs! could ye taste the mirth ye mar,
Not in the toils of glory would ye fret;
The hoarse dull drum would sleep, and man be
    happy yet.

George Byron *Childe Harolde*, Canto i, stanza 47 (1812)

Not a drum was heard, not a funeral note,
As his corse to the rampart we hurried;
Not a soldier discharged his farewell shot
O'er the grave where our hero we buried.

Charles Wolfe *The Burial of Sir John Moore after Corunna*
(1817)

'The sound of the drum drives out thought and for that
very reason it is the most military of instruments.'

Joseph Joubert *Pensées*, edited by **Chateaubriand** (1823)

The muffled drum's sad roll has beat
The soldier's last tattoo;
No more on Life's parade shall meet
The brave and fallen few.
On Fame's eternal camping-ground
Their silent tents are spread,

And Glory guards, with solemn round,
The bivouac of the dead.

Theodore O'Hara (1820–67)

Over there, over there, send the word, send the word
    over there!
That the Yanks are coming, the Yanks are coming,
The drum rum-tumming ev'rywhere:
So prepare, say a pray'r,
Send the word, send the word to beware!
We'll be over, we're coming over,
And we won't come back till it's over, over there!

George M. Cohan *Over There* (1917)

Dvořák, Antonin (1841–1904)

'The peasant in a frock-coat.'

Hans von Bülow

'Dvořák's *Requiem* bored Birmingham so desperately that
it was unanimously voted a work of extraordinary depth
and impressiveness, which verdict I record with a hollow
laugh, and allow the subject to drop by its own porten-
tous weight.'

George Bernard Shaw, quoted in **Hesketh Pearson**
Bernard Shaw: his Life and Personality (1942)

'If only I had been told that one could write a cello
concerto like that!'

Johannes Brahms, after hearing Dvořák's cello concerto

'The English owe a special debt to Dvořák. For at least a
hundred years before his arrival on our scene we had
been used to having most of our music written for us by
composers of foreign nationality ... Handel ... Chopin
... Hummel ... Moscheles ... Schumann, and above all
by Mendelssohn. But at the end of the eighteen seven-
ties, when Dvořák's Slavonic Dances took London by
storm, we were ready for the infusion of a new kind of
blood - for something in origin less sophisticated. The
popularity of his music here ... must be due to a
combination of the qualities which we as a nation like to
find in music: a clean, logical harmony; a rich,
homophonic melodiousness; a virile rhetoric ... and
lastly those fresh and homely emotions ... which are the
expression of a happy simple nature deriving at no far
remove from peasant stock.'

Edward Sackville-West and **Desmond Shawe-Taylor** *The
Record Guide* (1951)

Eastern Music . . . to Western Ears

'The colours of the day were ashy and wan. They were but the various tones of the heat. (It was like an Eastern melody, in the minor key, which exacerbates the nerves by its ambiguous monotony; and the ear waits impatiently a resolution, but waits in vain.)'

William Somerset Maugham 'The Force of Circumstance', in *The Casuarina Tree* (1926)

Einstein, Albert (1879–1955)

Einstein played the violin with some enthusiasm. He once played for Gregor Piatigorsky, the distinguished cellist, and he asked him: 'How well did I play?' Piatigorsky replied: 'You played *relatively* well.'

Elgar, Edward (1857–1934)

'He is furious with me for drastically cutting his A Flat Symphony – it's a very long work, the musical equivalent of the Towers of St. Pancras Station – neo-Gothic you know.'

Sir Thomas Beecham, in Neville Cardus *Sir Thomas Beecham: a Memoir* (1961)

'. . . indeed Elgar had often erred, though what is so often called his vulgarity is rather a kind of creative exuberance that can stop at nothing. He was singularly devoid of self criticism and welcomed with an almost childish delight any notion that would come to him, unbidden and as though simply snatched from the air, as he thought . . . he did not know clearly when he had written an inferior thing and when a masterpiece. . . . On the whole the vocal works are less sure of permanence than the instrumental, which finished with the mellow, autumnal cello concerto and three chamber works that were a new departure for Elgar at the very last – almost too late, yet their limpid tiredness is touching and unique . . . *Gerontius* struck a new note . . . even though oft-repeated festival experiences may have made the emotionally surcharged music a little oppressive.'

Eric Blom *Music in England* (1942)

'. . . the aggressive Edwardian prosperity that lends so comfortable a background to Elgar's finales is now as strange to us as the England that produced *Greensleeves*. . . . Stranger, in fact, and less sympathetic. In consequence much of Elgar's music, through no fault of its own, has for the present generation an almost intolerable air of smugness, self-assurance and autocratic benevolence.'

Constant Lambert *Music Ho!* (1934)

English Music

'These people have no ear, either for rhythm or music, and their unnatural passion for playing the piano and singing is therefore all the more repulsive. There is nothing on earth that is more terrible than English music, unless it be English painting.'

Heinrich Heine *Lutezia* (1843)

Etiquette

'It is the misfortune of musical people generally to be such enthusiasts, that, once beginning, they seldom know when to leave off: there are few things a greater *seccatura* than a long "Concerto", or duett upon the pianoforte, or an "Air with (endless) variations". The listeners get fidgetty and tired, although they are usually too polite to say so. I once sat next to a foreigner, who had endured with exemplary patience a tedious "Concerto", and who, when it was finished, applauded vehemently, then, turning round to me with a droll expression of countenance, said, *"perchè si finisce"* [Because it's finished.].

A song *now* and *then* is very desirable, as it is a relief to conversation, but half a dozen consecutively, even from St. Cecilia in person, would become a bore; besides which, people are now accustomed to hear popular songs executed by those whose profession it is, with a superiority rarely attainable in private life, so that amateurs seldom do more than provoke unfortunate comparisons. However, when highly-gifted musicians *are* found in private society, we have generally observed their *delicacy* to be in proportion to their *excellence*.

But the case is much worse when a professional "violinist" is admitted into a private party: he either flourishes away, unconscious that he is not in an orchestra, or else, desirous to prove his superiority over the "*dillettanti*", he overpowers them with a tone which might fill a cathedral. The best fiddles *scream* too much in (comparatively) small rooms, however delicately they may be played; besides that few even of the first English musicians seem to understand what an "*accompaniment*" really means, each performer being too intent on making his particular instrument heard above the rest, to care about the *subject*, or to feel that an "accompaniment" should be subdued, and *subservient* to the voice.

We once heard the silver tones of an exquisite singer completely destroyed, between the shriekings of a

48

fiddle, the vain-glorious grumblings of a violoncello, and the wheezings of a dyspeptic flute.'

Hints on Etiquette and The Usages of Society, with a Glance at Bad Habits (1836)

Ferrier, Kathleen (1912–53)

'I am doing [Gluck's] *Orfeo* here with an American Euridice, a Greek God of Love, a German producer and an Italian coach. Talk about the Tower of Babel! It is all in Italian and you can guess the job I'm having to learn the words from memory. . . . The stage manager has brought me a lyre of heavy plywood to get used to carrying it, and it's going to make a lovely weapon when the conductor tries me too far. One of these days he won't know what's hit him!'

Kathleen Ferrier, writing of rehearsing the role of Orfeo at Glyndebourne in 1947; quoted in **Winifred Ferrier** *The Life of Kathleen Ferrier* (1955)

Fiddle

'An instrument to tickle human ears by friction of a horse's tail on the entrails of a cat.'

Ambrose Bierce *The Devil's Dictionary* (1911)

Fife

'. . . the vile squealing of the wry-neck'd fife.'

William Shakespeare *The Merchant of Venice*, Act II, scene v (1596)

He thought he saw an Elephant,
That practised on a fife;
He looked again, and found it was
A letter from his wife.
'At length I realise', he said,
'The bitterness of Life!'

Lewis Carroll 'The Gardener's Song', *Sylvie and Bruno* (1889)

Flagstad, Kirsten (1895–1962)

'I have heard Toscanini conduct *Falstaff* and Flagstad sing Isolde – the only time that I cried at the Opera.'

A.J.P. Taylor *A Personal History* (1983)

Flute

'The flute is not an instrument which has a good moral effect; it is too exciting.'

Aristotle *Politics*, Book viii, chapter 6, section 5

'The sound of the flute will cure epilepsy, and a sciatic gout.'

Paracelsus-Theophrastus Bombastus von Hohenheim
Practica D. Theophrasti Paracelsi (1529)

The soft complaining flute
In dying notes discovers
The woes of hopeless lovers,
Whose dirge is whisper'd by the warbling lute.

John Dryden *Song for St Cecilia's Day* (1687)

'Soft as the breath of distant flutes at hours
When silent evening closes up the flowers.'

John Gay *Trivia*, Book ii (1716)

'Harmonides, a young flute player and scholar of Timotheus, at his first public performance, in order to *elevate* and *surprise*, began his solo with so violent a blast, that he *breathed his last breath into his flute*, and died upon the spot.'

Lucian (115–80), quoted in **Charles Burney** *A General History of Music* (1776)

In *David Copperfield* by Charles Dickens, Mr Mell, the Assistant Master at Salem House, collects David Copperfield from the stagecoach, and entertains him with his flute while he eats his breakfast, before setting out for his new school:
'The Master ... put his hand underneath the skirts of his coat, and brought out his flute in three pieces, which he screwed together, and began immediately to play. My impression is, after many years of consideration, that there never can have been anybody in the world who played worse. He made the most dismal sounds I have ever heard produced by any means, natural or artificial. I don't know what the tunes were – if there were such things in the performance at all, which I doubt – but the influence of the strain upon me was, first, to make me think of all my sorrows until I could hardly keep my tears back; then to take away my appetite; and lastly, to make me so sleepy that I couldn't keep my eyes open. They begin to close again, and I begin to nod, as the recollection rises fresh upon me.'

Charles Dickens *David Copperfield* (1849)

In *The Old Curiosity Shop* by Charles Dickens, Dick Swiveller, crossed in love, consoles himself upon his chosen instrument:

'Some men in his blighted position would have taken to drinking; but as Mr Swiveller had taken to that before, he only took, on receiving the news that Sophy Wackles was lost to him for ever, to playing the flute; thinking after mature consideration that it was a good, sound, dismal occupation, not only in unison with his own sad thoughts, but calculated to awaken a fellow feeling in the bosom of his neighbours. In pursuance of this resolution, he now drew a little table to his bedside, and arranging the light and a small oblong music-book to the best advantage, took his flute from its box, and began to play most mournfully.

The air was 'Away with melancholy' – a composition, which, when it is played very slowly upon the flute in bed, with the further disadvantage of being performed by a gentleman but imperfectly acquainted with the instrument, who repeats one note a great many times before he can find the next, has not a lively effect. Yet for half the night, or more, Mr Swiveller, lying sometimes on his back with his eyes upon the ceiling, and sometimes half out of bed to correct himself by the book, played this unhappy tune over and over again; never leaving off, save for a minute or two at a time to take breath ... and then beginning again with renewed vigour. It was not until he had quite exhausted his several subjects of meditation, and had breathed into his flute the whole sentiment of the purl down to its very dregs, and had nearly maddened the people of the house, and at both the next doors, and over the way, – that he shut up the music-book, – extinguished the candle, and finding himself greatly lightened and relieved in his mind, turned round and fell asleep.

He awoke in the morning, much refreshed; and having taken half an hour's exercise at the flute, and graciously received a notice to quit from his landlady, who had been in waiting on the stairs for that purpose since the dawn of day, repaired to Bevis Marks.'

Charles Dickens *The Old Curiosity Shop* (1841)

A velvet flute note fell down pleasantly
Upon the bosom of that harmony . . .
Somewhat, half song, half odour, forth did float
As if a rose might somehow be a throat.

Sidney Lanier *The Symphony* (1877)

Foster, Stephen (1826–64)

'That was the greatest tragedy of his life: his utter incapacity to exploit his genius as it deserved. Ingenuous, impractical, maladjusted to his environment, given to dreams and fancies that carried him away from reality, he was incapable of looking after himself. He wasted his life as well as his genius; and his closing days saw him an impoverished drunkard in the gutters of New York's Bowery.'

David Ewen *Songs of America* (1978)

'This is really folk music, despite the known authorship of Foster's melody and verse – folk art, which the American people have taken to themselves as their own.'

Olin Downes, in **Irene Downes**, ed: *Olin Downes on Music* (1957)

Frederick II, King of Prussia (1712–86)

'If you are under the impression that the king loves music you are wrong. He only loves the flute. And more than that – the only flute he loves is his own.'

One of Frederick the Great's court musicians (attrib)

French Songs

In Oscar Wilde's comedy *The Importance of Being Earnest* Lady Bracknell relied on Algernon to arrange the programme of music at her dinner party. Music, as he explains, is very important, but it is important to have the right kind of music: 'If one plays good music, people don't listen, and if one plays bad music people don't talk. . . .' She thanks him for his help, and adds:

'It is very thoughtful of you. . . . I'm sure the programme will be delightful, after a few expurgations. French songs I cannot possibly allow. People always seem to think that they are improper, and either look shocked, which is vulgar, or laugh, which is worse. But German sounds a thoroughly respectable language, and indeed, I believe is so. . . .'

Oscar Wilde *The Importance of Being Earnest* (1895)

Fugue

'One damn fiddle after another.'

H.L. Mencken

'Any dolt can write a fugue a day; some do; but if, musically speaking, he is of feeble mind his best-made fugue will never be anything but a piece of doltish music.'

Ernest Newman, in *The Sunday Times* (7 March 1943)

Furtwängler, Wilhelm (1886–1954)

Furtwängler's concept of beautiful sound (*Klangschönheit*) may have been profound, his musical intelligence may have been immense, his soul gigantic – and all the rest of it, but orchestral players agree that his gestures, movements and general choreography were extraordinary, and his stick technique notoriously difficult to follow. When he first conducted at Florence, his bodily movements amazed the players, one of whom called out: 'Coraggio, Maestro!' by way of well-intentioned encouragement.

Toscanini and Furtwängler seriously quarrelled over the latter's failure to take a strong stand against Nazism. Furtwängler's reputation was so unsavoury that even though he was offered the post of succeeding Toscanini at the New York Philharmonic Orchestra in 1936, he had to turn it down because of American Jewish opinion. In 1938 he went to the Glyndebourne Festival to see Verdi's *Macbeth*. Unfortunately, Toscanini was also there:
  'Toscanini's visit to *Macbeth* was something of a headache for the Glyndebourne management. It was only by much clever diplomatic manoeuvring that he was somehow kept from catching sight of Furtwängler who had come to the same performance and, as a Nazi musician, was the Italian conductor's particular *bête noir*.... A gossip writer reported that at *Macbeth* "Furtwängler applauded with a certain professional respect, Toscanini with an enthusiasm worthy of any amateur".'

Spike Hughes *Glyndebourne: a History of the Festival Opera* (1965)

German Singers

'A German singer! I should as soon expect to get pleasure from the neighing of my horse.'

Frederick II, King of Prussia; quoted in *The Frank Muir Book* (1976)

Gershwin, George (1898–1937)

'... a sort of musical kaleidoscope of America – of our vast melting-pot, of our incomparable national pep, our blues, our metropolitan madness.'

George Gershwin, writing of his own music

'From Gershwin emanated a new American music not written with the ruthlessness of one who strives to demolish established rules, but based on a new native gusto and wit and awareness. His was a modernity that reflected the civilization we live in as excitingly as the headline in today's newspaper.'

Ira Gershwin, quoted in **Edward Jablonski** and **Lawrence D. Stewart** *The Gershwin Years* (1958)

'A creature of the glitter and tinsel of Tin Pan Alley, Broadway, Hollywood, and the news media, he also hobnobbed with some of the most important names in serious music and was often the object of their admiration. Gershwin was a living, breathing, striving, plotting mass of contradictions – always on the run, always out to conquer the world, always seeking the adulation of the vast, unknown public. . . . He was a child of his age who never became old enough to outlive his usefulness.'

Charles Schwartz *Gershwin: his Life and Music* (1973)

In the winter of 1932–33 Dashiell Hammett returned from Hollywood and told Edmund Wilson that the Gershwins (Ira and George) had 'wanted something special' while they worked in Hollywood:

'so they got a house with three grand pianos in the living room, six mandarin coats over the couch. Artificial moonlight by electric lamps from outside the windows; busts of Mozart facing out the windows. Barbecue stand where they first put a table in your car, then decided they weren't giving enough service, so they added a movie screen with talkies and a small organ. . . .'

Edmund Wilson *The Thirties – From Notebooks and Diaries of the Period* (1980)

Gibbons, Orlando (1583–1625)

'The subjects of Orlando Gibbons's madrigals are so simple and unmarked, that if they were now to be executed by instruments alone, they would afford very little pleasure to the greatest friends of his productions, and those of the same period. At the time they were published, however, there was nothing better with which to compare them, and the best music which good ears can obtain, is always delightful, till better is produced.'

Charles Burney *A General History of Music* (1776)

Gluck, Christoph Willibald (1714–87)

'Gluck knew no more of counterpoint than my cook does.'

George Frideric Handel

Gluck made his will in 1786. He left his soul to the infinite mercy of God, and bequeathed 25 florins for 50 masses for his soul; other bequests included:

'... to the poor house one florin, to the General Hospital, one florin, to the Bürger Hospital one florin, to the Normal School, one florin – four florins in all.'

Glyndebourne

'Today the upper-middle classes, liking their opera sugar-coated, regard Glyndebourne as the smart thing to go to. They particularly enjoy picnicking with other middle-class people and writing down the names of the more attractive herbaceous plants in the garden on their programme.... There is a mile-long queue for the loo in the interval, while all those who pretend to know the opera backwards mug up on the synopsis for the next act.'

Jilly Cooper *Class* (1979)

Gounod, Charles (1818–93)

Gounod's *Faust*, first performed in Paris on 19 March 1859, was one of the most successful operas of the 19th century. Charles Dickens saw it in Paris on 31 January 1863, and the story of the temptation of a beautiful and innocent young girl by an older man moved him deeply, possibly because at that time he was experiencing the great crisis in his emotional life, the climax of which was to lead to his deserting his wife, Catherine, and living with a young actress, Ellen Ternan. He wrote to Georgina Hogarth, his wife's sister, that he was passionately and personally moved by 'that noble and sad story, so nobly and sadly rendered'. Mephistopheles was 'surrounded by an infernal red atmosphere of his own ... and Marguerite by a pale blue mournful light. The two never blending. After Marguerite has taken the jewels placed in her way in the garden, a weird evening draws on, and the bloom fades from the flowers, and the leaves of the trees droop and lose their fresh green, and mournful shadows overhang her chamber window, which was innocent and gay at first. I couldn't bear it, and gave in completely....' In a later letter to Georgina he wrote: 'I could hardly bear the thing, it affected me so, and sounded in my ears so like a mournful echo of things that lie in my own heart'.

Charles Dickens, letters dated 1 and 12 Feb 1863

Grieg, Edvard (1843–1907)

'At the Grieg Concert, St. James's Hall. A crowded house, mainly filled with hordes of those idle, well-dressed, supercilious, unintelligent women who inhabit the West End and the more expensive suburbs. . . .

Grieg came on in a short jacket of black velvet which served to decrease still further his short stature. He has a large head with white hair and a bald patch, and the shrewd wrinkled face of a thinker. A restless man, weary and yet the victim of an incurable vivacity. The concussion of his hands on the keys jerked back his head at every chord. Between the movements of a sonata he bowed almost imperceptibly and wiped his face every time with the same mechanical movement. He looked like one who has exhausted the joys of fame and of being adored.'

Arnold Bennett *Journals*, entry for 22 Nov 1897

Grisi, Giulia (1811–69)

'. . . saw Grisi in [Bellini's] *Il pirata*, and the passion and fire of a scene between her, Mario, and Fornasari, was as good and great as it is possible for anything operatic to be. They drew on one another, the two men – not like stage-players, but like Macready himself [William Charles Macready, a celebrated actor]; and she, rushing in between them; now clinging to this one, now to that, making a sheath for their naked swords with her arms, now tearing her hair in distraction as they broke away from her and plunged again at each other; was prodigious.'

Charles Dickens, after hearing *Il pirata* in Paris in 1844, in a letter to his biographer John Forster; quoted in **J. Forster** *The Life of Charles Dickens* (1872–4)

Guitar

'Nothing is more beautiful than a guitar, except, possibly, two.'
Fryderyk Chopin

Hallé, Sir Charles (1819–95)

Charles Hallé, the pianist and conductor, was often invited to play at fashionable London parties. On one occasion the best people in society were well represented and tongues and teacups were busy as he sat down at the piano. The clatter ceased for a while as he began to play, but gradually recommenced and rose in a crescendo. As he ended, he was applauded and congratulated by all present. He was asked to play again some time later, with the same effect. Quiet to begin with, and then chattering and clattering throughout. He played a third solo towards the end of the party, and again faced considerable competition. The hostess was very voluble in her appreciation of his musicianship.

'But nobody listened!' said Hallé.

'Sir Charles!' exclaimed the hostess, rather shocked. 'Not even Your Ladyship. Or you would have noticed that I played the same piece each time.'

Handel, George Frideric
(1685–1759)

'A city company's barge was employed for the musick, where fifty instruments of all sorts, played all the finest symphonies, composed express for this occasion, by Mr. Handel: which His Majesty liked so well that he caused it to be played over three times in going and returning. At eleven, His Majesty went ashore at Chelsea where a supper was prepared, and then there was another fine consort of music which lasted until 2: after which His Majesty came again into his barge and returned the same way, the musick continuing to play until he landed.'

On the first performance of the *Water Music*, on the River Thames on 17 July 1717, in the *London Daily Courant* (19 July 1717)

'On Tuesday last Mr. Handel's Sacred Grand Oratorio, *The Messiah* was performed in the New Music Hall in Fishamble Street; the best judges allowed it to be the most finished piece of Music. Words are wanting to express the exquisite delight it afforded to the admiring crowded audience. The sublime, the grand, and the tender, adapted to the most elevated, majestic and moving words, conspired to transport and charm the ravished heart and ear. It is but justice to Mr. Handel that the world should know he generously gave the money arising from this grand performance, to be equally shared by the Society for relieving Prisoners, the Charitable Infirmary, and Mercer's Hospital, for which they will ever gratefully remember his name; and that the Gentlemen of the Two Choirs (Christ Church and St. Patrick's) Mr. Duburg, Mrs. Avolio, and Mrs. Cibber, who all performed their parts to admiration acted also on the same disinterested principle, satisfied with the deserved applause of the public, and the conscious pleasure of promoting such useful and extensive charity. There were above 700 people in the room, and the sum collected amounted to about £400, out of which £127 goes to each of the three great and pious charities.'

On the first performance of *Messiah*, on 13 April 1742 in Dublin, in *Faulkner's Journal*

'He was the greatest composer that ever lived. I would uncover my head, and kneel before his tomb.'

Ludwig van Beethoven; quoted in **Percy M. Young** *Handel* (1947)

During the mid-19th century, when large choral societies were beginning to flourish and Handel was much in vogue, there developed a fashion for performing his choral works with massive forces; such performances were particularly associated with the Crystal Palace.

'June 20th. 1857. All this past week the world has been occupied with the Handel Concerts at the Crystal Palace, which went off with the greatest success and *éclat*. I went to the first ('Messiah'), and the last ('Israel in Egypt'); they were amazingly grand, and the beauty of the *locale*, with the vast crowds assembled in it, made an imposing spectacle. The arrangements were perfect, and nothing could be easier than the access and egress, or more comfortable than the accommodation. But the wonderful assembly of 2,000 vocal and 500 instrumental performers did not produce musical effect so agreeable and so perfect as the smaller number in the smaller space of Exeter Hall. The volume of sound was dispersed and lost in the prodigious space, and fine as it undoubtedly was, I much prefer the concerts of the Harmonic Society.'

Charles Greville *A Journal of the Reign of Queen Victoria from 1852–1860* **2** (1887)

'Handel is only fourth rate. He is not even interesting.'

Pyotr Il'yich Tchaikovsky

'The urge to create was so tyrannical that it ended by isolating him from the rest of the world.... His brain was never idle; and whatever he might be doing, he was no longer conscious of his surroundings. He had a habit of speaking so loudly that everybody learned what he was thinking. And what exaltation, what tears, as he wrote! He sobbed aloud when he was composing the aria *He was despised*.... This huge mass of flesh was shaken by fits of fury. He swore almost with every phrase.... When his choirs were inattentive he had a way of shouting *Chorus!* at them in a terrible voice that made the public jump ... at the rehearsals of his oratorios at Carlton House ... if the Prince and Princess of Wales did not appear punctually, he took no trouble to conceal his anger; and if the ladies of the Court had the misfortune to talk during the performance he was not satisfied with cursing and swearing, but addressed them furiously by name....'

'He was part of England's patrimony, and the British lion walked beside him.'

Romain Rolland *A Musical Tour through the Land of the Past* (1922)

'In Bach's Cantatas, as in his Passions and Oratorio, one never thinks of the theatre, whereas in Handel one does: he is much more of a showman ... Bach never is, although he can reach a much higher plane of emotion. In the science of obtaining effects Handel was a great master, maybe the greatest. Bach never thought of an effect: his music came out of the most intimate part of his mind and never aimed at anything but the purest.'

Pablo Casals, quoted in **J.M. Corredor** *Conversations with Casals* (1956)

'He wrote Italian music better than any Italian, French music better than any Frenchman, English music better than any Englishman, and, with the single exception of Bach, outrivalled all other Germans.'

Sir Thomas Beecham

Harmony

The melting voice through mazes running,
Untwisting all the chains that tie
The hidden soul of harmony.

John Milton *L'Allegro* (1632)

First was the world as one great cymbal made,
Where jarring winds to infant nature played;
All music was a solitary sound,
To hollow rocks and murmuring fountains bound.

Jubal first made the wilder notes agree,
And Jubal tunèd Music's jubilee;
He called the echoes from their sullen cell,
And built the organ's city, where they dwell.

Each sought a consort in that lovely place,
And virgin trebles wed the manly bass,
From whence the progeny of numbers new
Into harmonious colonies withdrew;

Some to the lute, some to the viol went,
Others chose the cornet eloquent.
These practising the wind, and those the wire,
To sing man's triumphs, or in Heaven's quire.

Then music, the mosaic of the air,
Did of all these a solemn noise prepare,
With which she gained the empire of the ear,
Including all between the earth and sphere.

Victorious sounds! yet here your homage do
Unto a gentler conqueror than you;
Who, though he flies the music if his praise,
Would with you Heaven's hallelujahs raise.

Andrew Marvell (1621–78) *Music's Empire*

Harmony

When such music sweet
Their hearts and ears did greet,
As never was by mortal finger struck,
Divinely-warbled voice
Answering the stringed noise,
As all their souls in blissful rapture took:
The Air such pleasure loth to lose,
With thousand echoes still prolongs each heav'nly close.

Nature that heard such sound
Beneath the hollow round
Of *Cynthia's* seat, the Airy region thrilling,
Now was almost won
To think her part was done,
And that her reign had here its last fulfilling;
She knew such harmony alone
Could hold all Heav'n and Earth in happier union.

At last surrounds their sight
A Globe of circular light,
That with long beams the shame-fac'd night array'd,
The helmed Cherubim
And sworded Seraphim,
Are seen in glittering ranks with wings displayed,
Harping in loud and solemn choir,
With unexpressive notes to Heav'ns new-born Heir.

Such Music (as 'tis said)
Before was never made,
But when of old the sons of morning sung,
While the Creator Great
His constellations set,
And the well-balanc'd world on hinges hung,
And cast the dark foundations deep,
And bid the weltering waves their oozy channel keep.

Ring out ye Crystal spheres,
Once bless our human ears,
(If ye have power to touch our senses so)
And let your silver chime
Move in melodious time;
And let the Base of Heav'ns deep Organ blow,
And with your ninefold harmony
Make up full consort to th'Angelic symphony.

For if such holy Song
Enwrap our fancy long,
Time will run back, and fetch the age of gold,
And speckl'd vanity
Will sicken soon and die,
And leprous sin will melt from earthly mould,
And Hell itself shall pass away,
And leave her dolorous mansions to the peering day.

John Milton *Ode on the Morning of Christ's Nativity* (1629)

Harp

Old times were changed, old manners gone,
A stranger filled the Stuarts' throne;
The bigots of the iron time
Had called his harmless art a crime.
A wandering Harper, scorned and poor,
He begged his bread from door to door,
And tuned, to please a peasant's ear,
The harp a King had loved to hear.

Sir Walter Scott *The Lay of the Last Minstrel* (1805)

The harp that once through Tara's halls
The soul of music shed,
Now hangs as mute on Tara's walls
As if that soul were fled,
So sleeps the pride of former days,
So glory's thrill is o'er,
And hearts that once beat high for praise
Now feel that pulse no more.

No more to chiefs and ladies bright
The harp of Tara swells;
The chord alone that breaks at night
Its tale of ruin tells.
Thus Freedom now so seldom wakes,
The only throb she gives,
Is when some heart indignant breaks,
To show that still she lives

Thomas Moore *The Harp That Once Through Tara's Halls* (1834) (Tara was the capital of Ireland in the early Middle Ages, when the Irish nation was a great centre of European learning and civilization.)

'If you have pretty hands and arms, there can be no objection to your playing on the harp if you play well.'

Advice to Young Ladies, in *Enquire Within upon Everything* (1860)

Harpsichord

'It was Mr. Western's custom every afternoon, as soon as he was drunk, to hear his daughter play on the harpsichord; for he was a great lover of music, and perhaps, had he lived in town, might have passed for a connoisseur; but he always excepted against the finest compositions of Mr. Handel. He never relished any music but what was light and airy; and indeed his most favourite tunes were Old Sir Simon the King, St. George he was for England, Bobbing Joan, and some others.

His daughter, though she was a perfect mistress of music, and would never willingly have played any but Handel's, was so devoted to her father's pleasure, that she learnt all those tunes to oblige him. However, she would now and then endeavour to lead him into her own taste; and when he required the repetition of his ballads, would answer with a "nay, dear Sir;" and would often beg him to suffer her to play something else.'

Henry Fielding *Tom Jones* Book iv, chapter 5 (1749)

Question: Pray, what musical instrument was used by our ancestors before the introduction of the piano?
Answer: The harpsichord, an instrument somewhat similar, but very inferior in tone.

The Child's Guide to Knowledge: Being a Collection of Useful and Familiar Questions and Answers on Every-day Subjects, Adapted for Young Persons and Arranged in the Most Simple and Easy Language by a Lady (1842)

Haydn, Franz Joseph (1732–1809)

Haydn's 'Military' Symphony, no.100, caused a sensation when it was first performed during Johann Peter Salomon's subscription concerts at the Hanover Square Rooms, London. The second movement was singled out for special comment, with its bass drum, cymbals, trumpets and triangle – all colourful 'military' effects:

'. . . it is the advancing battle; and the march of men, the sounding of the charge, the thundering of the onset, the clash of arms, the groans of the wounded, and what may well be called the hellish roar of war increase to a climax of horrid sublimity! which, if others can conceive, he alone [Haydn] can execute; at least he alone hitherto has effected these wonders.'

Morning Chronicle (9 April 1794)

'I had the fortune to be a witness of the deep emotion and the most lively enthusiasm that several performances of this oratorio [*The Creation*] under Haydn's own direction wrought in all hearers. Haydn also confessed to me that he could not convey the feelings that mastered him when the performance wholly matched his wishes, and the audience in total silence listened intently to every note. "Now I would be ice cold in my whole body, now a burning fever would come over me, and I was afraid more than once that I should suddenly suffer a stroke."'

Georg August Griesinger, translated in **Vernon Gotwals** *Joseph Haydn: Eighteenth-century Gentleman and Genius* (1963)

'It is my last child, but it still looks like me.'

Joseph Haydn, of his last composition, the unfinished String Quartet op.103, which consists only of an Andante and a Minuet

Henze, Hans Werner (born 1926)

'My passion for music began when I was about 13. From then on I neglected my school work to play music in the afternoons and evenings, and to compose chamber pieces that were sightread once with friends and then laid aside. I did not like practising the piano. Everything was still a game. Just as puddles became lakes for children, domestic cats turn into tigers, and teachers into evil spirits, so my fellow-players became *beaux* and geniuses. But making music with them became a reality that penetrated the secret of the world, and in which there were formulations at last for what had hitherto been inexpressible. The suspended cadences in the adagios of Corelli's "church" sonatas were ceremonious promises of love, full of renunciation; the allegros in Bach, Vivaldi and Bach-Vivaldi represented sexual excitement. In the closing chorus of the *St Matthew Passion* we, the chosen children, sat down in actual tears after the long evening of lamentation.'

Hans Werner Henze *Music and Politics – Collected Writings 1953–81* (1982)

Hérold, Ferdinand (1791–1833)

Hérold became famous as an opera composer, especially for his comic operas *Zampa* (1831) and *Le pré aux clercs* (1832). As he lay dying he remarked that he was going too soon: 'I was just beginning to understand the stage.'

Horn

'[in spite of its] imperfections, it is of all wind instruments the most beautiful in respect of timbre and intrinsic quality of tone, while the feelings aroused by its charm are generally admitted to be irresistible.'

Louis François Dauprat (1781–1868), the horn virtuoso and teacher, in his horn tutor (1824); quoted in *Musical Instruments through the Ages*, edited by **Anthony Baines** (1961)

The horn, the horn, the lusty horn
Is not a thing to laugh to scorn.

William Shakespeare *As You Like It*, Act IV, scene ii (1599)

'Mr. Bramble had not time to make his remarks upon the agreeable nature of this serenade [the bells of Bath Abbey], before his ears were saluted with another concert that interested him more nearly. Two negroes, belonging to a Creole gentleman, who lodged in the same house, taking their station at a window in the staircase, about ten feet from our dining-room door, began to practise upon the French-horn; and being in the very first rudiments of execution, produced such discordant sounds, as might have discomposed the organs of an ass – You may guess what effect they had upon the irritable nerves of uncle; who, with the most admirable expression of splenetic surprise in his countenance, sent his man to silence these dreadful blasts, and desire the musicians to practise in some other place, as they had no right to stand there and disturb all the lodgers in the house. Those sable performers, far from taking the hint, and withdrawing, treated the messenger with great insolence ... in the meantime they continued their noise, and even endeavoured to make it more disagreeable; laughing between whiles, at the thoughts of being able to torment their betters with impunity.'

Tobias Smollett *Humphry Clinker* (1771)

Each day I gird my feeble soul with prayer:
May then the blood of Bayard be my own:
May I ride hard and straight and smite him square,
And in a clash of arms be overthrown;
And as I fall hear through the evening air
The distant horn of Roland, faintly blown.

Frederick F. Van de Water (born 1890) *The Last Tourney*

Samuel Johnson attended a Freemason's funeral at Rochester 'and some solemn musick being played on French-horns' caused him to remark: 'This is the first time that I have ever been affected by musical sounds ... the impression made upon me was of a melancholy sound'. His companion, Bennet Langton, added that the effect was a fine one, to which Johnson answered: 'Yes, if it softens the mind so as to prepare it for the reception of salutary feelings, it may be good: but inasmuch as it is melancholy *per se*, it is bad'.

James Boswell *The Life of Samuel Johnson* (1791)

Humperdinck, Engelbert (1854–1921)

'At first I thought I should be a second Beethoven; presently I found that to be another Schubert would be good; then, gradually, satisfied with less and less, I was resigned to be a Humperdinck.'

Engelbert Humperdinck, quoted in **John W. Klein** 'Engelbert Humperdinck: a Centennial Appreciation', *Opera* (1954)

Italian Music

'I don't think I shall ever become a convert to Italian music. It's such trash.'

Richard Strauss, after his first visit to the Italian opera at Rome, in a letter of 1886; quoted in **Willi Schuh** *Richard Strauss: a Chronicle of the Early Years 1864–1898* (1982)

'Music is yet but in its nonage, a forward child, which gives hope of what it may be hereafter in *England*, when the masters of it shall find more encouragement. 'Tis now learning *Italian*, which is its best master, and studying a little of the *French* air, to give it somewhat more gaiety and fashion. Thus being further from the sun, we are of later growth than our neighbour countries, and must be content to shake off our barbarity by degrees.'

Henry Purcell, in the preface to his semi-opera on Thomas Betterton's *The History of Dioclesian* (1690)

Italian Opera

'I saw an Italian Opera in music, the first that had been in England of this kind.'

John Evelyn *Diary*, entry for 5 Jan 1674

In his biography of John Hughes (1677–1719) Dr Johnson put forward his celebrated opinion of Italian opera:

'In 1703 his *Ode on Music* was performed at Stationers' Hall; and he wrote afterwards six cantatas, which were set to music by the greatest master of that time [Handel], and seem intended to oppose or exclude the Italian opera, an exotic and irrational entertainment, which has always been combated, and always has prevailed.'

Samuel Johnson *Lives of the English Poets* Volume I (1779)

'The spacious appearance of the Italian Opera-House, the brilliancy of the audience, (particularly the display of full-dressed persons in the pit,) and the comforts of the CORINTHIAN's box, afforded JERRY much delight and satisfaction. "But," said HAWTHORN, "it appears to me that the company, generally, value this theatre more for a lounging fashionable place of meeting with each other than to listen to the performances; and the great mass of the spectators, I believe, are also in the dark as to a *conversant* knowledge of the dialogue. To *look* and to be *looked at*, to be superbly attired, as leaders, on the one side, as well as numerous persons on the other to follow the fashions, are features of a more prominent description: however, it is most certainly a brilliant spectacle, and I have no doubt but many persons of superior *taste* visit the Opera-House for no other purpose but the gratification they feel at the talents displayed by the performers. The dancing, I confess, is so truly elegant that I want words to express my admiration of it. But, my dear Coz." said JERRY, laughing, "to have one's box at the Opera, you know, is quite the *ton!*" "I have no fault to find with your portrait of this fashionable *picture* of LIFE IN LONDON," replied TOM; "at least, the outline is good; and, instead of any prejudice being exhibited against the Italian Opera, I think it ought to be viewed as a stimulus towards the improvement of our male and female singers: and, without any disparagement or illiberality, I consider the English performers now as powerful rivals."'

Pierce Egan *Life in London; or, the Day and Night Scenes of Jerry Hawthorn Esquire and his elegant Friend Corinthian Tom, accompanied by Bob Logic the Oxonian in their Rambles and Sprees through the Metropolis* (1821)

'In the opera house of Italy there gathered an audience which passed its evenings in amusement; part of this amusement was formed by the music sung upon the stage, to which one listened from time to time in pauses of the conversation; during the conversation and visits paid from box to box the music still went on, and with the same office as one assigns to table music at grand dinners, namely, to encourage by its noise the otherwise timid talk. The music which is played with this object, and during this conversation, fills out the virtual bulk of an Italian operatic score; whereas the music which one really listens to makes out perhaps a twelfth part thereof. An Italian opera must contain at least *one* aria to which one is glad to listen: if it is to have a success, the conversation must be broken, and the music listened to with interest, at least six times; whilst the composer who is clever enough to attract the audience's attention a whole twelve times is lauded as an inexhaustible melodic genius. . . .'

Richard Wagner 'The Music of the Future', in *Richard Wagner's Prose Works* **3**, edited by W.A. Ellis, (1894)

Ives, Charles (1874–1954)

'Ives is nothing if not a nationalistic American composer. The forces conveyed by his music are deeply, typically American. They are the essences of a practical people, abrupt and nervous and ecstatic in their movements and manifestations – brought into play with a certain reluctance and difficulty, but when finally loosed, jaggedly, abruptly, almost painfully released, with something of an hysteric urgency; manifested sometimes in a religious and mystical elevation, but almost invariably in patterns that have a paroxysmal suddenness and abruptness and violence.'

Paul Rosenfeld, quoted in **Herbert A. Leibowitz** *Musical Impressions: Selections from Paul Rosenfeld's Criticism* (1969)

Karajan, Herbert von (born 1908)

'Karajan is a kind of musical Malcolm Sargent.'
Sir Thomas Beecham

Kleiber, Erich (1890–1956)

Kleiber's direction of Richard Strauss's *Der Rosenkavalier* is legendary. Posterity may be grateful that it was recorded. Those who heard it in person may justly regard themselves among the blessed of the earth. Some insight may be gained from pondering some critical and analytic points made about Kleiber's art as an operatic director:

'*Der Rosenkavalier* is loved, of course, for its great lyric scenes, but it is primarily a narrative opera, in which the conductor's task is that of setting an over-all tempo, and his second that of getting the words across without robbing the orchestra of the animal resources with which Strauss had endowed it.... By never dwelling on moments of deep emotion he alienated those who liked to lie in *Rosenkavalier* as others lie in a pine-bath. By keeping the orchestra down to a genuine *piano* and *pianissimo* he gave people more to listen to than they had expected to hear. And by bringing out the inner parts ... he altogether transcended the impact, inauthentic and gross, on which people had come to rely. Certain passages ... had, it is true, a Handelian fullness: but they also had a Handelian fleetness of mind, and that is not what people expect of *Der Rosenkavalier*....

But it is by the great lyrical moments that *Rosenkavalier* is remembered. The humour may go never so well, but if the heart is not touched, the evening's traffic will seem long indeed. Kleiber did not subscribe to the *larmoyant* view. 'Comedy', Strauss and Hofmanstahl had called it, and comedy it remains in Kleiber's recording.... Kleiber's conduct of the opera is throughout a lesson in the uses of reserve – provided, of course, that the reserve comes from a superabundance of feeling.'
John Russell *Erich Kleiber: a Memoir* (1957)

Klemperer, Otto (1885–1973)

'If I thought I knew the part, I realized my mistake within the first five pages. Klemperer sat at the piano like an evil spirit, thumping on it with long hands like a tiger's claws, and dragging my terrified voice into the vortex of his fanatical will. Elsa's dreamy serenity became a rapturous ecstasy; her timorous pleading a challenging demand. For the first time I felt my inhibiting shyness fall away and I sank into the flame of inner experience. I had always wanted to sing like this.'
Lotte Lehman, describing being rehearsed in Wagner's *Lohengrin* in 1912; quoted in **Peter Heyworth** *Otto Klemperer: his Life and Times, vol.1: 1885–1933* (1983)

Klemperer particularly loathed the modern tendency for young musicians, pianists, conductors and so on, to praise one anothers' work extravagantly. He commented:

'In my day, Furtwängler, Bruno Walter and Kleiber and I *hated* each other! It was more healthy.'

Quoted in *The Tongs and the Bones: the Memoirs of Lord Harewood* (1981)

'One day ... the elderly Klemperer tottered onto the platform, stood for a moment in acknowledgement of the audience's welcome, then turned to the orchestra, perched on his conductor's stool – and unwittingly exposed an expanse of shirt through his open fly.

In vain the players tried to draw his attention to it. The hall was hushed ... the symphony began ... continued ... developed ... ended magnificently. At long last the orchestra leader managed to attract the old man's attention.

"Maestro!" he hissed, "Your fly buttons! They are undone!"

Klemperer regarded him with a mixture of disbelief and amazed contempt.

"Vot has dat to do wiz Beethoven?" he demanded.'

Steve Race *Dear Music Lover* (1981)

Lessons and Teachers

'A vile beastly rottenheaded foolbegotten brazenthroated pernicious priggish screaming, tearing, roaring, perplexing, splitmecrackle crashmecriggle insane ass of a woman is practising howling below-stairs with a brute of a singing master so horribly that my head is nearly off.'

Edward Lear, in a letter to Lady Strachey of 24 Jan 1859

'Insist upon you neither piping nor fiddling yourself. It puts a gentleman in a very frivolous, contemptible light; brings him into a great deal of bad company; and takes up a great deal of time, which might be much better employed.'

Lord Chesterfield, in a letter to his son

Librettos

'You must begin by pleasing the actors and actresses; you must satisfy the musical composer; you must consult the scene painter. . . .

The three principal personages of the drama ought to sing five airs each; two in the first act, two in the second, and one in the third. The second actress and the second soprano can have only three; and the inferior characters must be satisfied with a single air each, or two at the most.... You must observe the same precaution in distributing the bravura airs, the airs of action, the inferior airs, and the minuets and rondeaus ... avoid giving impassioned airs, bravura airs, or rondeaus, to inferior actors. Those poor devils must be satisfied with what they get, and every opportunity of distinguishing themselves is denied them.'

Carlo Goldoni (1707–93), writing to a would-be operatic librettist; quoted in **George Hogarth** *Memoirs of the Musical Drama* (1838)

'Nothing is capable of being well set to music that is not nonsense.'

Joseph Addison (1672–1719), *The Spectator*

Liszt, Franz (1811–86)

'Most of all he gives me the impression of being a spoilt child. He is good, over-bearing, amiable, arrogant, noble and generous, often hard with others.... Liszt can play as he likes. And the result is always full of interest even if one can often find faults of taste particularly in his compositions which I cannot qualify in any other term than "awful".... I am very near to detesting him as a composer, but as a virtuoso he has sent me into a transport of admiration.'

Clara Schumann, talking to her husband **Robert Schumann** after giving a concert with Liszt in December 1841

During their relationship, George Sand would often be upstairs writing while Liszt was downstairs composing. She would hear the opening bars of some strange new theme which crossed his mind, which he would play, and then suddenly abandon, leaving the musical fragments: 'with one leg in the air, dancing in space like clubfooted imps'.

George Sand (1804–76), journals

'Turn your eyes to any one composition that bears the name of Liszt, if you are unlucky enough to have such a thing on your pianoforte, and answer frankly, if it contains one bar of genuine music. Composition indeed! decomposition is the proper word for such hateful fungi, which choke up and poison the fertile plains of harmony, threatening the world with drought.'

Musical World (30 June 1855)

'A venerable man with a purple nose: a Cyrano de Cognac nose.'

James Gibbons Huneker *Old Fogy*

The prodigious gifts with which he was endowed were such as to encourage in him the character of actor or magician. When this is taken into consideration it is surprising how little he was spoiled by adulation. His transformation into a priest was the result of sincere religious feeling. The generosity of his character proved itself in his support of so many younger musicians: Dvořák, Grieg, Borodin, Tchaikowsky. All things considered, Liszt must remain one of the phenomena of music. As a pianist he has never been equalled; he is a great, if neglected, composer; and he ranks with Byron among the most striking figures of the whole Romantic epoch.

Sacheverell Sitwell *Liszt* (1934)

'Liszt was the first to insist on the complete independence of the fingers. When he played he did not use the wrist and the hand only, but also employed the articulations of the elbow and shoulder, including the arms, which were thus set free; he crossed them over, leaping from bass to treble at a speed like that of a conjuring trick. Movements of the torso which, hitherto, had been kept rigid, were part of a technical scheme to distribute the flow of movement of the arms and fingers, even to the back of the pianist; his whole body expressed his emotion.'

Emile Haraszti 'Liszt et la musique hongroise', in *La musique des origines à nos jours*, edited by N. Dufourcq (1946)

Lully, Jean-Baptiste (1632–87)

Lully was born in Florence and was of Italian origin, as master of music at the court of Louis XIV he instituted many reforms and innovations, including opera-ballets and organising military music for Louis' armies He is singled out for special praise by Voltaire:

'The arts which do not solely depend upon the intellect had made but little progress in France before the period which is known as the age of Louis XIV. Music was in its infancy; a few languishing songs, some airs for the violin, the guitar and the lute, composed for the most part in Spain, were all that we possessed. Lully's style and technique were astonishing. He was the first in France to write bass counterpoint, middle parts, and figures. At first some difficulty was experienced in his playing his compositions, which now seem so easy and simple. At the present day there are a thousand people who know music, for one who knew it in the time of Louis XIII; and the art has been perfected by this spread of knowledge. Today, there is no great town which has not its public concerts: yet at that time Paris itself had

none; the King's twenty-four violins comprised the sum
total of French music.'

Voltaire *The Age of Louis XIV* (1751), translated by **Martyn
P. Pollack** (1926)

Lute

Now westward *Sol* had spent the richest beams
Of noon's high glory, when hard by the streams
Of *Tiber*, on the scene of a green plat,
Under the protection of an oak; there sate
A sweet Lutes-master; in whose gentle airs
He lost the day's heat, and his own hot cares.
    Close in the covert of the leaves there stood
A Nightingale, come from the neighbouring wood . . .
There stood she listening, and did entertain
The music's soft report; and mould the same
In her own murmurs, that whatever mood
His curious fingers lent, her voice made good:
The man perceived his rival, and her art,
Dispos'd to give the light-foot lady sport
Awakes his lute, and 'gainst the fight to come
Informs it, in a sweet *Praeludium*
Of closer strains, and ere the war begin,
He lightly skirmishes on every string
Charg'd with a flying touch: and straightway she
Carves out her dainty voice as readily,
Into a thousand sweet distinguish'd tones,
And reckons up in soft divisions,
Quick volumes of wild notes; to let him know
By that shrill taste, she could do something too.
    His nimble hands instinct then taught each string
A cap'ring cheerfulness; and made them sing
To their own dance; now negligently rash
He throws his arm, and with a long drawn dash
Blends all together; then distinctly trips
From this to that; then quick returning skips
And snatches this again, and pauses there.
She measures every measure, every where
Meets art with art. . . .

Richard Crashaw *Music's Duel* (1617)

                    One morning early
This accident encountered me: I heard
The sweetest and most ravishing contention,
That art and nature ever were at strife in . . .
A sound of music touched mine ears, or rather
Indeed, entranced my soul: as I stole nearer,
Invited by the melody, I saw
This youth, this fair faced youth, upon his lute,
With strains of strange variety and harmony,
Proclaiming, as it seemed, so bold a challenge
To the clear choristers of the woods, the birds,
That, as they flocked about him, all stood silent,

Wondering at what they heard. I wondered too.
 . . . A nightingale,
Nature's best skilled musician, undertakes
The challenge, and for every several strain
The well shaped youth could touch, she sung her own;
He could not run division with more art
Upon his quaking instrument, than she,
The nightingale, did with her various notes
Reply to . . .
For they were rivals, and their mistress, harmony.
Some time thus spent, the young man grew at last
Into a pretty anger, that a bird
Whom art had never taught clefts, moods, or notes,
Should vie with him for mastery, whose study
Had busied many hours to perfect practice:
To end the controversy, in a rapture
Upon his instrument he plays so swiftly,
So many voluntaries, and so quick,
That there was curiosity and cunning,
Concord in discord, lines of differing method
Meeting in one full centre of delight . . .
The bird, ordained to be
Music's first martyr, strove to imitate
These several sounds: which, when her warbling throat
Failed in, for grief, down dropped she on his lute,
And brake her heart! It was the quaintest sadness,
To see the conqueror upon her hearse,
To weep a funeral elegy of tears . . .
He looked upon the trophies of his art,
Then sighed, then wiped his eyes, then sighed and cried:
'Alas poor creature! I will soon revenge
This cruelty upon the author of it;
Henceforth this lute, guilty of innocent blood,
Shall never more betray a harmless peace
To an untimely end:' and in that sorrow,
As he was pashing it against a tree,
I suddenly stepped in.

John Ford *The Lover's Melancholy* I i (1629)

'Luting and singing take away a manly stomach . . . these
instruments make a mans wit so soft and smooth, so
tender and queazy, that they be less able to brook strong
and tough study.'

Roger Ascham *The Scholemaster* (1570)

. . . Do the sounds
Which slumber in the lute, belong alone
To him who buys the chords?

Friedrich von Schiller *Don Carlos*, Act IV, scene xxi (1787)

If thou would'st have me sing and play
As once I play'd and sung,
First take this time-worn lute away,
And bring one freshly strung.

Thomas Moore *If thou Wouldst Have me Sing and Play*
(1834)

When Orpheus strikes the trembling lyre,
The streams stand still, the stones admire;
The list'ning savages advance,
The wolf and lamb around him trip,
The bears in awkward measures leap,
And tigers mingle in the dance:
The moving woods attended as he play'd,
And Rhodolphe was left without a shade.

Joseph Addison *A Song for St Cecilia's Day* (1712)

MacDiarmid, Hugh (1892–1978)

Come, follow me into the realm of music. Here is
    the gate
Which separates the earthly from the eternal.
It is not like stepping into a strange country
As we once did. We soon learn to know everything there
And nothing surprises us any more. Here
Our wonderment will have no end, and yet
From the very beginning we feel at home.

At first you hear nothing, because everything sounds.
But now you begin to distinguish between them. Listen.
Each star has its rhythm and each world its beat.
The heart of each separate living thing
Beats differently, according to its needs,
And all the beats are in harmony.

Your inner ear grows sharper. Do you hear
The deep notes and the high notes?
They are immeasurable in space and infinite as
    to number.
Like ribbons, undreamt-of scales lead from one world
    to another,
Steadfast and eternally moved.
More wonderful than those miraculous isles of Greece
'Lily on lily, that o'erlace the sea,'
Than the marvellous detailed intensity of Chinese life,
Than such a glimpse as once delighted me of the
    masterly and exhaustive

Hugh MacDiarmid *Plaited Like the Generations of Men*

see also Busoni, Ferruccio Benvenuto

McCormack, John (1884–1945)

After a production of *Madama Butterfly* McCormack told
the tenor who had played Lieutenant Pinkerton:
    'You sang very well, but you must have been a rotten
naval officer.'
    'Why?' demanded the other.
    'You began with a little bit of gold braid on your

sleeve,' explained the Irishman. 'Then years later, when you return to Japan and your little Butterfly, you're still wearing the same bit of braid. Don't you ever get promoted? When I sang Pinkerton, I took good care to promote myself to Commander in the third act.'

Charles Neilson Gattey *The Elephant that Swallowed a Nightingale and other Operatic Wonders* (1981)

Mahler, Gustav (1860–1911)

'A symphony must be like the world. It must contain everything.'

Gustav Mahler, speaking to **Jean Sibelius**

In the summer of 1910 Mahler, distressed about his relationship with his wife, was advised to consult Sigmund Freud. The composer and the distinguished psychoanalyst met at a hotel in Leyden:

'. . . and then spent four hours strolling through the town and conducting a sort of psycho-analysis. Although Mahler had no previous contact with psychoanalysis, Freud said he had never met anyone who seemed to understand it so swiftly. . . . In the course of the talk Mahler suddenly said that now he understood why his music had always been prevented from achieving the highest rank through the noblest passages, those inspired by the most profound emotions, being spoiled by the intrusion of some common-place melody. His father, apparently a brutal person, treated his wife very badly, and when Mahler was a young boy there was a specially painful scene between them. It became quite unbearable to the boy, who rushed away from the house. At that moment, however, a hurdy-gurdy in the street was grinding out the popular Viennese air *"Ach, Du lieber Augustin"*. In Mahler's opinion the conjunction of high tragedy and light amusement was from then on inextricably fixed in his mind, and the one mood inevitably brought the other with it.'

Ernest Jones *The Life and Work of Sigmund Freud*, edited and abridged by Lionel Trilling and Steven Marcus (1961)

'. . . what I heard was not what I had expected to hear. First of all, in spite of a slack, under-rehearsed and rather apologetic performance, the scoring startled me. It was mainly "soloistic" and entirely clean and transparent. The colouring seemed calculated to the smallest shade, and the result was wonderfully resonant. I wasn't bored for one of its forty-five minutes. . . . The form was so cunningly contrived; every development surprised one and yet sounded inevitable. Above all, the material was remarkable, and the melodic shapes highly original, with such rhythmic and harmonic tension from beginning to end. After that ... I made every effort to hear Mahler's music, in England and on the continent, on the radio and on the gramophone, and in my enthusiasm, I began a great crusade among my friends on behalf of my new god – I must admit with only average success.'

Benjamin Britten, after hearing a Mahler symphony to which he had not looked forward to listening; quoted in **Michael Kennedy** *Britten* (1981)

Mary, Queen of Scots (1542–87)

Mary had a deep love of music, which appealed to the moody and romantic side of her character. She was a skilled player of the lute and virginals, on which she loved displaying her celebrated long white fingers. She also had a fine singing voice. Musical talent played a significant role in her selection of personal servants – she chose David Rizzio because he was a musician. In 1561 it is recorded she had five viols players and three lutenists, and several of her valets of the bedchamber played and sang: 'so that Mary could beguile the long dark Scottish winter evenings, with the sort of little musical supper parties which she had enjoyed in France. The Queen also loved to have music to accompany her Mass; at first this presented a problem, since the chapel organs had been destroyed at the time of the Reformation as being profane instruments.'

Antonia Fraser *Mary Queen of Scots* (1969)

Melody

'Composers should write tunes that chauffeurs and errand boys can whistle.'

Sir Thomas Beecham, in the *New York Times* (9 March 1961)

'The language of tones belongs equally to all mankind, and melody is the absolute language in which the musician speaks to every heart.'

Richard Wagner *Beethoven*

Mendelssohn, Felix (1809–47)

'It was in the beginning of May 1821, when walking in the streets of Berlin with my master and friend, Carl Maria von Weber, he directed my attention to a boy, apparently about eleven or twelve years old, who, on perceiving the author of *Freischütz*, ran towards him, giving him a most hearty and friendly greeting. '"Tis Felix Mendelssohn", said Weber, introducing me at once to the prodigious child, of whose marvellous talent and execution I had heard so much at Dresden. I shall never forget the impression of that day on beholding that beautiful youth, with his auburn hair clustering in ringlets round his shoulders, the ingenuous expression of his clear eyes, and the smile of innocence and candour on his lips. He would have it that we should go with him at once to his father's house; but as Weber had to attend a rehearsal, he took me by the hand, and made me run a race till we reached his home. Up he went briskly to the drawing room, where, finding his mother, he exclaimed: ''Here is a pupil of Weber's, who knows a great deal of his music of the new opera. Pray, mamma, ask him to play it for us!'' and so, with an irresistible impetuosity, he pushed me to the pianoforte, and made me remain there until I had exhausted all the store of my recollections. When I then begged of him to let me hear some of his own compositions, he refused, but played from memory such of Bach's fugues or Cramer's exercises [Johann Baptist Cramer (1771–1858)] as I could name. At last we parted, but not without a promise to meet again.'

Sir Julius Benedict *A Sketch of the Life and Works of the late Felix Mendelssohn* (1850)

'We went into the deep twilight to the Palace of Holyrood where Queen Mary lived and loved . . . the chapel is roofless . . . I believe I found today in that old chapel the beginning of my Scottish Symphony.'

Felix Mendelssohn in a letter written during a visit to Scotland in 1829

To the noble artist, who, surrounded by the Baal-worship of corrupted art, has been able by his genius and science to preserve faithfully, like another Elijah, the worship of true art, and once more to accustom our ear, lost in the world of an empty play of sounds, to the pure notes of expressive composition and legitimate harmony; to the great master, who, makes us conscious of the unity of his conception through the whole maze of his creation, from the soft whispering to the mighty raging of the elements – written in token of grateful remembrance, by

ALBERT
Buckingham Palace,
April 24th. 1847.

Prince Albert, in a score of *Elijah* which he presented to Mendelssohn, after hearing the work (with Queen Victoria) performed by the Sacred Harmonic Society at Exeter Hall on 23 April 1847

'I am very happy here, and enjoy myself very much – especially when I can shut my eyes and ears to music and musicians – which is fortunately not difficult. Were I to tell them my opinion of their music-making they would think me rude, and were I to speak to them of music in general they would think me quite mad. So I do not trouble them with my ideas, but wander about looking at the splendid life of this city and her streets ... buying a bunch of lilies-of-the-valley from some bawling old woman in the crowd, and finding in it more music than in all the concerts which I survived yesterday, shall endure tomorrow, and put up with again on Friday. Of the English style of singing I shall say nothing, but will give you a sample in December – you will fall off your chair laughing. ...'

Felix Mendelssohn, in a letter to Eduard Devrient (a German baritone) from England in 1829–30

'I once heard Mendelssohn conduct Beethoven's Eighth Symphony at a concert-rehearsal in Berlin. I noticed that he would pick out a detail here and there – almost at random – and polish it up with a certain pertinacity, which did such excellent service for the detail that I could only wonder why he did not pay the same attention to other nuances. ... With regard to conducting, he personally told me that a too slow tempo was the devil, and that for choice he would rather things were taken too fast. A really good performance was a rarity at any time, but with a little care one might gloss things over, and this could best be accomplished by never dawdling, and by covering the ground at a good, stiff pace.'

Richard Wagner 'On Conducting', in *Richard Wagner's Prose Works*, edited and translated by **William Ashton Ellis 4** (1895)

Mengelberg, Willem (1871–1951)

'Beethoven, like many other composers, sometimes made changements in his scores, even after publication, and then he also was deaf. So vy not the conductor also, who often knows mooch better than the composer? I vos de best pupil of Svhindler, who vos the best pupil of Beethoven, zo I know vat Beethoven meant. ...'

Willem Mengelberg, quoted in **Bernard Shore** *The Orchestra Speaks* (1938)

Meyerbeer, Giacomo (1791–1864)

'To startle or tickle is Meyerbeer's favourite rule, and one he carries out successfully with the rabble. It is one and the same time calculated and empty, superficial and "deep". Unfortunately it is impossible to deny that he has some wit, and we also know that he possesses an entire treasury of forms. One can recognize Rossini, Mozart, Hérold, Weber, Bellini, even Spohr – in short, the whole of music. Truly, let us thank heaven that

nothing worse can come after this, unless we turn the
stage into a gallows.'

Robert Schumann, writing about Meyerbeer's opera *Les
Huguenots*

'He was like the starling who follows the ploughshare
down the field, and merrily picks up the earthworm just
uncovered in the furrow. Not one departure is his own,
but each he has eavesdropped from his forerunner,
exploiting it with monstrous ostentation; and so swiftly
that the man in front has scarcely spoken a word, than *he*
has bawled out the entire phrase, quite unconcerned as
to whether he has caught the meaning of that word;
whence it has generally arisen that he has actually said
something slightly different from what the man in front
intended. But the noise of the Meyerbeerian phrase was
so deafening that the man in front could no longer arrive
at bringing out his own real meaning: willy-nilly, if only
to get a word in edgeways, he was forced at last to chime
into that phrase. In Germany alone was Meyerbeer
unsuccessful, in his search for a new fledged phrase to fit
anyhow the word of Weber: what Weber uttered from
the fill of his melodic life could not be echoed in the
lessoned, arid formalism of Meyerbeer. At last, dis-
gusted with the fruitless toil, he betrayed his friend by
listening to Rossini's siren strains, and departed for the
land where grew those raisins. Thus he became the
weathercock of European opera music, the vane that
always veers at first uncertain with the shift of wind, and
comes to a standstill only when the wind itself has
settled on its quarter. Thus Meyerbeer in Italy composed
operas *à la* Rossini, precisely till the wind of Paris began
to chop, and Auber and Rossini with their *Muette de
Portici* and *William Tell* blew the gale into a storm! With
one bound was Meyerbeer in Paris!'

Richard Wagner 'Opera and Drama', in *Richard Wagner's
Prose Works* **2** (1893)

Milhaud, Darius (1892–1974)

Milhaud was a pupil of Charles Widor (1844–1937).
Listening to a dissonant work of Milhaud's, Widor said:
'The worst of it is that one gets used to it.'

Military Music

Farewell the plumed troops, and the big wars
That makes ambition virtue! O farewell!
Farewell the neighing steed and the shrill trump,
The spirit-stirring drum, th' ear-piercing fife,
The royal banner, and all quality,
Pride, pomp and circumstance, of glorious war!

William Shakespeare *Othello*, Act III, scene iii (1604)

'All the delusive seduction of martial music.'

Fanny Burney *Diary*, part viii (1802)

'Every morning, about eleven o'clock, the band of the Guards assembles in the courtyard of that miserable palace of St. James's, and plays for about three quarters of an hour, – softly – slowly – in that beautiful medium, the *sotto voce* of the Italians, which, both for instruments and voices, is so full, so rich, so favourable to great effects in music. The performers are mostly Germans. The audience is usually composed of the lower ranks of people – the higher are not up.'

Louis Simond *Journal of a Tour in Great Britain*, entry for 2 June 1810

'So far as I know, though it has been for so long one of the spectacles most familiar to inhabitants of London, and most loved by visitors, little has been written about the Changing of the Guard. . . . First, the new Guard marches to the ceremony, just as later the old Guard returns to barracks, to the military music of the drums and fifes of the battalion from which it is drawn. . . . The drill exhibited has many of the merits of a work of art. . . . But of all the difficult tasks, the Ensign – the youngest officer present – has the most awkward . . . he must lower the Colour in salute to the Colour of the King's Guard relieving or being relieved, and hold it stretched out in that position for some twenty paces. Many weeks of practice . . . are required before perfection is attained . . . in this stately ceremonial crawl to the solemn and inspiring strains of the March from Handel's *Scipio*, which the Grenadiers have adopted as their own, in the same way that the Coldstream use the March from *Figaro*. . . . For some twenty minutes or half an hour . . . the band would lift the spirits of the watching crowd, ox-eyed at the railings. . . .'

Osbert Sitwell *Great Morning* (1948)

Mitropoulos, Dimitri (1896–1960)

'The Mitropoulos concerts were wholly dependable technically. Musically they varied a good deal. Some of them were nervous and violent, others calm almost to the point of platitude. . . . He is a great workman, certainly. He is an interesting musician, certainly. The exact nature of his musical culture and personality remains, however, vague. He seems to be oversensitive, overweening, overbrutal, overintelligent, underconfident, and wholly without ease. He is clearly a musician of class, nevertheless, and a coming man of some sort in the musical world.'

Virgil Thomson, writing of Mitropoulos's first concerts with the New York Philharmonic Orchestra, in the *Herald Tribune* (1946)

Monteux, Pierre (1875–1964)

Monteux used to tell the orchestras he conducted, usually in their first rehearsal together: 'There is no use playing jokes on me, *mes enfants*, I made them all myself long before you were thought of. *Alors*, forget it, and let's work'. But on one memorable occasion they really had him:

'Only once did the San Francisco Orchestra really play a good joke on him by substituting a Spike Jones record, one of the loudest, in place of the required dulcet nightingale song recording used in the *Pines of Rome* suite of Respighi. He roared with laughter.'

Doris Monteux *It's All in the Music: the Life and Work of Pierre Monteux* (1965)

More, Sir Thomas (1478–1535)

In *Utopia*, Sir Thomas More describes the use made of music in worship in his ideal society:

'Then they sing praises unto God, which they intermix with instruments of music, for the most part of other fashions than these that we use in this part of the world. And like as some of ours be much sweeter than theirs, so some of theirs do far pass ours. But in one thing doubtless they go exceeding far beyond us. For all their music, both that they play upon instruments and that they sing with man's voice, doth so resemble and express natural affections, the sound and tune is so applied and made agreeable to the thing, that whether it be a prayer or else a ditty of gladness, of patience, of trouble, of mourning or of anger, the fashion of the melody doth so represent the meaning of the thing that it doth wonderfully move, stir, pierce and inflame the hearers' minds.'

Thomas More *Utopia* (1515–16)

Mozart, Wolfgang Amadeus (1756–91)

In 1771 Mozart may well have applied to join Archduke Ferdinand's household as a court musician. The archduke wrote to his mother, the Empress Maria Theresia, for her advice, and she wrote in reply:

'I do not know where you can place him, since I feel that you do not require a composer, or other useless people. But if it would give you pleasure, I have no wish to prevent you. What I say here is only meant to persuade you not to load yourself down with people who are useless, and to urge you not to give such people the right to represent themselves as being in your service. It gives one's service a bad name when such types go about the world like beggars; besides, he has a large family.'

'Whether the angels play only Bach in praising God I am not quite sure; I am sure, however, that *en famille* they play Mozart.'

Karl Bath, in the *New York Times* (11 Dec 1968)

'The musical talent may well show itself earliest of any; for music is something innate and internal, which needs little nourishment from without, and no experience drawn from life. Really, however, a phenomenon like that of Mozart remains an inexplicable prodigy. But how would the Divinity find everywhere opportunity to do wonders, if he did not sometimes try his powers on extraordinary individuals, at whom we stand astonished, and cannot understand whence they come?'

Johann Wolfgang von Goethe, in a conversation recorded on 14 Feb 1831; quoted in *Conversations of Goethe with Eckermann and Soret*, translated by **John Oxenford** (1874)

During the rehearsals for the first production of *Don Giovanni* at Prague in 1787, there was some difficulty in getting Signora Bondi, who was singing the role of Zerlina, to scream in the right manner and the right place as she is seized by Don Giovanni:

'It was tried repeatedly and failed. At length, Mozart, desiring the orchestra to repeat the piece, went quietly on the stage, and awaiting the time that she was to make the exclamation, grasped her so suddenly and so forcibly, that, really alarmed, she shrieked in good earnest. He was now content. "That's the way", said he, praising her, "You must cry out just in that manner."'

Edward Holmes *The Life of Mozart* (1845)

At a production of *Don Giovanni* at the Vienna State Opera in 1958, the lift which was supposed to take the bass Cesare Siepi down to hell, below stage, got stuck halfway, with Don Giovanni clearly visible from the chest up. Two attempts failed to haul the arch-seducer off to the nether regions. Then a voice in Italian from the audience said: 'Oh my God, how wonderful! Hell is full!'

Hugh Vickers *Great Operatic Disasters* (1979)

Le nozze di Figaro was first performed in Britain in spring 1812, amid the military and political upheaval in Europe and the crisis at home brought about by the severe mental illness of George III:

'Mozart's standard opera of Figaro was performed last

night with a strength of musical talent which has seldom been displayed at one time at this or any other theatre. Mrs. Dickons (Countess) seemed to be animated with a spirit of rivalship, which produced exertions far beyond what we have ever witnessed, even from this charming singer. The surprise which this new display of her powers excited drew down thunders of applause at the close of almost every cadence ... at the end of the performance M. Tramezzani came forward and sang "God Save the King". He was joined in the chorus by the whole of the audience, most of whom testified their loyalty by shedding tears. The Duke of Cambridge who was present was particularly affected at this display of public affection for his venerable Sire, and was himself strongly agitated by the same emotions.'

The Sun (17 May 1812)

Just before his last illness Mozart was commissioned, in somewhat mysterious circumstances, to write a Requiem Mass. He began work on it, but it was never to be finished. During his last illness his opera *Die Zauber-flöte* was given its first performance, in Vienna, where Mozart was Konzertmeister to the archbishop; he is said to have followed the opera with his score as he lay in bed, watch in hand. 'Now the first act is over ... now is the time for the Queen of the Night. . . .' The music of the Requiem was the last he heard:

'The next day he was worse, and he felt that his end was fast approaching. He said to Constance: "Oh, that I could only once more hear my 'Flauto Magico!'" About two o'clock he was visited by three intimate friends, to whom he showed the score of the *Requiem.* After giving Süssmayr (his pupil) his final directions with regard to it, he once again glanced through it; and with tears in his eyes, exclaimed: "Did I not tell you that I was writing it for myself?" He then expressed a wish to have it sung. . . . Mozart took the alto part, and his friends the three remaining ones. They proceeded as far as the Lacrymosa, when suddenly Mozart burst into tears, and the score was put aside. He then fell into a delirium from which he never rallied. . . . He died on 5th December 1791. His body was wrapped in the black dress of the Masonic Brotherhood and he was buried in a common grave in the churchyard of St. Mark, near Vienna. When his wife, Constance, and a few friends came some time after to erect a cross over it, they were unable to identify the place where Mozart's remains actually lay.'

Frederick Crowest *The Great Tone Poets* (1891)

'Mozart's loss is irreparable. I shall never in my life forget his clavier playing. It touched the heart!'

Joseph Haydn, quoted in **Georg August Griesinger** *Biographische Notizen über Joseph Haydn*, translated by Vernon Gotwals (1963)

Music

'Music and rhythm find their way into the secret places of the soul. . . . Musical innovation is full of danger to the state, for when modes of music change, the laws of the state always change with them.'

Plato *The Republic*, Book iii (*c* 380 BC)

'Men imitated with their mouths the liquid warblings of birds long before they were able to join together in singing melodious songs . . . it was the whistling of the zephyr in the cavities of reeds that first taught country-folk to blow into hollow stalks. Then, little by little, they learned the sweet notes that ripple from the plaintive flute as the player's fingers strike the stops. . . . With this music they would soothe and charm their hearts, after they had eaten their fill. . . .'

Lucretius *De rerum natura* Book V (*c* 58 BC)

'Music is the medicine of a troubled mind.'

Walter Haddon *Lucubrationes poemata: De musica* (1567)

If music be the food of love, play on;
Give me excess of it, that, surfeiting,
The appetite may sicken, and so die,
That strain again! It had a dying fall:
O, it came o'er my ear like the sweet sound,
That breathes upon a bank of violets,
Stealing, and giving odour!

William Shakespeare *Twelfth Night*, Act I, scene i (1599)

'It is proportion that beautifies everything, this whole universe consists of it, and music is measured by it.'

Orlando Gibbons *The First Set of Madrigals and Mottets* (1612)

'Many and sundry are the means which philosophers and physicians have prescribed to exhilarate a sorrowful heart, to divert those fixed and intent cares and meditations, which in this malady so much offend; but, in my judgement, none so present, none so powerful, none so apposite, as a cup of strong drink, mirth, music, and merry company . . . [music has the quality] not only to expell the greatest griefs, but it doth extenuate fears and furies, appeaseth cruelty, abateth heaviness; and, to such as are watchfull, it causeth quiet rest; it takes away spleen and hatred, be it instrumental, vocal, with strings, wind . . . and it cures all irksomeness and heaviness of the soul. Labouring men, that sing to their work, can tell as much; and so can soldiers when they go to fight, whom terror of death cannot so much affright, as the sound of trumpet, drum, fife, and such like music animates. . . . It makes a child quiet, the nurse's song;

and many times the sound of a trumpet on a sudden, bells ringing, a boy singing some ballad tune early in the street, alters, revives, recreates a restless patient that cannot sleep in the night. In a word it is so powerful a thing that it ravisheth the soul ... the queen of the senses, by sweet pleasure (which is a happy cure;) and corporal tunes pacify our incorporeal soul ... and carries it beyond itself, helps, elevates, extends it. Scaliger [Julius Caesar Scaliger (1484–1558)] gives a reason of these effects, because the spirits about the heart take in that trembling and dancing air into the body, are moved together and stirred up with it, or else the mind, as some suppose, harmonically composed, is roused up at the tunes of music. And 'tis not only men that are so affected, but almost all other creatures. You know the tale of Hercules Gallus, Orpheus, and Amphion ... that could make stocks and stones, as well as beasts and other animals, dance after their pipes; the dog and hare, wolf and lamb ... stood all gaping upon Orpheus; and trees, pulled up by the roots, came to hear him.... Arion made fishes follow him, which, as common experience evinces, are much affected with music. All singing birds are much pleased with it, especially nightingales ... and bees among the rest, though they be flying away when they hear any tingling sound, will tarry behind. Harts, hinds, horses, dogs, bears, are exceedingly delighted with it....'

Robert Burton *The Anatomy of Melancholy* (1621)

'Tunes and airs, even in their own nature, have in themselves some affinity with the affections.... So it is no marvel if they alter the spirits. Yet generally music feedeth that disposition of the spirits which it findeth.'

Francis Bacon *Sylva sylvarum*, Century ii, section 114 (1626)

'Music strikes in me a deep fit of devotion, and a profound contemplation of the First Composer. There is something in it of Divinity more than the ear discovers.'

Sir Thomas Browne *Religio medici*, Part ii, section 9 (1642)

Milton advocated the therapeutic use of music in his discussion of education. He perceived music as having a significant part to play in aiding recreation between academic work and physical activities; after fencing and wrestling, students would find the experience of music greatly beneficial:

'The interim of unsweating themselves regularly, and convenient rest before meat may both with profit and delight be taken up in recreating and composing their travailed spirits with the solemn and divine harmonies of music heard, or learned; either while the skilful Organist plies his grave and fancied descant in lofty fugues, or the whole Symphony with artful and unimaginable touches adorn and grace the well-studied chords of some choice composer; sometimes the Lute, or soft organ-stop waiting on elegant voices either to Religious, martial, or civil ditties; which if wise men and prophets be not extremely out, have great power over dispositions and manners, to smooth and make them gentle from rustic harshness and distempered passions.'

John Milton *Tractate of Education* (1644)

'Music is nothing else but wild sounds civilized into time and tune.'

Thomas Fuller *A History of the Worthies of England* (1662)

'With my wife to the King's House to see *The Virgin Martyr* [a tragedy by Massinger and Dekker of 1622], the first time it hath been acted a great while; and it is mighty pleasant; not that the play is worth much, but it is finely acted by Beck Marshall. But that which did please me beyond anything in the whole world, was the wind-music when the angel came down; which is so sweet that it ravished me, and indeed, in a word, did wrap up my soul so that it made me really sick, just as I have formerly been when in love with my wife; that neither then, nor all the evening going home, and at home, I was able to think of any thing but remained all night transported, so as I could not believe that ever any music hath that real command over the soul of a man as this did upon me; and makes me resolve to practice wind-music, and to make my wife do the like.'

Samuel Pepys *Diary*, entry for 27 Feb 1667

Music's the cordial of a troubled breast,
The softest remedy that grief can find;
The gentle spell that charms our care to rest
And calms the ruffled passions of the mind.
   Music does all our joys refine,
   And gives the relish to our wine.

John Oldham *An Ode on St Cecilia's Day* (1683)

Some beauties yet no precepts can declare,
For there's a happiness as well as care.
Music resembles poetry: in each
Are nameless graces which no methods teach
And which a master-hand alone can reach.
If, where the rules not far enough extend,
(Since rules were made but promote their end)
Some lucky licence answer to the full
The intent proposed, that licence is a rule.

Alexander Pope *An Essay on Criticism* (1709)

'How is that of the three arts which imitate nature, the one with the most arbitrary and least precise expression speaks most strongly to the soul? Would it be the case that in showing objects less, it leaves more scope for the imagination?'

Denis Diderot (1713–84)

'Music is the only sensual pleasure without vice.'

Samuel Johnson, quoted in **Sir John Hawkins** *Johnsonia* (1787–9)

There is in souls a sympathy with sounds,
And, as the mind is pitch'd, the ear is pleas'd
With melting airs, or martial, brisk, or grave:
Some chord in unison with what we hear
Is touch'd within us, and the heart replies.

William Cowper *The Task*, Book 6 (1785)

'Music does not ... express this or that particular and definite joy, this or that sorrow, or pain, or horror, or delight ... but joy, sorrow, pain, delight *themselves*.'

Arthur Schopenhauer *The World as Will and Idea* (1819)

'Who is there that, in logical words, can express the effect music has on us? A kind of inarticulate unfathomable speech, which leads us to the edge of the Infinite, and lets us for moments gaze into that!'

Thomas Carlyle *On Heroes, Hero-Worship and the Heroic in History* (1841)

'See deep enough, and you see musically; the heart of nature being everywhere music, if you can only reach it.'

Thomas Carlyle *Heroes and Hero-worship*, Lecture 3 (1841)

'When music affects us to tears, seemingly causeless, we weep *not*, as Gravina supposes, from "Excess of pleasure"; but through excess of an impatient, petulant sorrow that, as mere mortals, we are as yet in no condition to banquet upon those supernal ecstasies of which the music affords us merely a suggestive and indefinite glimpse.'

Edgar Allan Poe 'Music', in *Democratic Review* (1844)

'The sentiments deducible from the conception of sweet sound simply, are out of the reach of analysis – although referable, possibly, in their last result, to that merely mathematical recognition of *equality* which seems to be *the root of all Beauty*. Our impressions of harmony and melody in conjunction, are more readily analyzed; but one thing is certain – that the *sentimental* pleasure derivable from music, is nearly in the ratio of its indefinitiveness. Give to music any undue *decision* –

imbue it with any very *determinate* tone – and you deprive it, at once, of its ethereal, its ideal, and, I sincerely believe, of its intrinsic and essential character. You dispel its dream-like luxury; – you dissolve the atmosphere of the mystic in which its whole nature is bound up: – you exhaust it of its breath of faëry.'

Edgar Allan Poe 'Song Writing', in *Southern Literary Messenger* (April 1849)

'Music is well said to be the speech of angels.'

Thomas Carlyle *Essays: the Opera* (1854)

'There is no music in Nature, neither melody or harmony. Music is the creation of man.... Emotion, not thought, is the sphere of music; and emotion quite as often precedes as follows thought.'

H.R. Haweis *Music and Morals* (1871)

'Music is a means of giving form to our inner feelings without attaching them to events or objects in the world.'

George Santayana *Little Essays* (1920)

'music is, by its very nature, powerless to *express* anything at all, whether a feeling, an attitude of mind, a psychological mood, a phenomenon of nature etc. ... if, as is nearly always the case, music appears to express something, this is only an illusion, and not a reality.'

Igor Stravinsky *An Autobiography* (1936)

'Music can be made anywhere, is invisible, and does not smell.'

W.H. Auden *In Praise of Limestone* (1951)

'Music, not being made up of objects nor referring to objects, is intangible and ineffable; it can only be, as it were, inhaled by the spirit: the rest is silence.'

Jacques Barzun, ed: *The Pleasures of Music* (1951)

'In one sense, emotion conveyed through music is more real than that conveyed through the other arts – because it is more pure.... The true expressive difference between the arts is that painting conveys feeling through a visual image, and literature through a rationally intelligible statement, but music conveys the naked feeling direct.'

Deryck Cooke *The Language of Music* (1959)

'When we separate music from life we get art.'

John Cage *Silence* (1961)

Music

'A verbal art like poetry is reflective; it stops to think. Music is immediate, it goes on to become.'

W.H. Auden 'Notes on Music and Opera', in *The Dyer's Hand* (1962)

'The trouble with music appreciation in general is that people are taught to have too much respect for music; they should be taught to love it instead.'

Igor Stravinsky, in *New York Times Magazine* (27 Sept 1964)

'Music is a language by whose means messages are elaborated, that such messages can be understood by the many, but sent out only by the few, and that it alone among all the languages unites the contradictory character of being at once intelligible and untranslatable – these facts make the creator of music a being like the gods, and make music itself the supreme mystery of human knowledge.'

Claude Lévi-Strauss *Mythologiques I: Le cru et le cuit* (1964)

'Music exists – not on canvas nor yet on the staff – only in motion. The good listener will hear it as the present prolonged. . . . If music could be translated into human speech, it would no longer need to exist.'

Ned Rorem *Music from Inside Out* (1967)

'The education of the ear is fifty years behind the education of the eye. We are still hostile to sounds that surprise us. Bad music always sounds pleasant, but good music makes you gnash your teeth.'

Pierre Boulez, in *Esquire* (1969)

'Too many pieces (of music) finish too long after the end.'

Igor Stravinsky, quoted in *New York Review of Books* (1971)

'Music . . . can name the unnamable and communicate the unknowable.'

Leonard Bernstein *The Unanswered Question* (1976)

'Music creates order out of chaos.'

Yehudi Menuhin, in an interview in *The Sunday Times* (1976)

'There are two musics . . . the music one listens to, the music one plays. These two musics are two totally different arts, each with its own history, its own sociology, its own aesthetics, its own erotic; the same composer can be minor if you listen to him, tremendous if you play him (even badly) – such is Schumann.

The music one plays comes from an activity that is very little auditory, being above all manual (and thus in a way much more sensual). It is the music which you or I can play . . . with no other audience than its participants. . . . This music has disappeared; initially the province of the idle (aristocratic) class, it lapsed into an insipid social rite with the coming of the democracy of the bourgeoisie (the piano, the young lady, the drawing room, the nocturne) and then faded out altogether. . . . To find practical music in the West, one has to look to another public . . . (the young generation, vocal music, the guitar). Concurrently, passive, receptive music, sound music is become *the* music (that of concert, festival, record, radio). . . . In short, there was first the actor of music, then the interpreter . . . then finally the technician, who relieves the listener of all activity . . . and abolishes in the sphere of music the very notion of *doing*.'

Roland Barthes *Image – Music – Text* (1977)

'Music is the human treatment of sounds.'

Jean-Michel Jarre, in an interview in 1978

'The function of music is to release us from the tyranny of conscious thought. Music first and last should sound well, should allure and enchant the ear. Never mind the inner significance.'

Sir Thomas Beecham *Beecham Stories* (1978)

Music is an ocean that covers the world,
An element that lets you drown in air.
It moves beyond time, rocks with rhythm,
Speaks for itself with sweet tongued tunes,
With a weird wordless eloquence,
With a primitive chaotic power.
It is everywhere,
International in tone,
Atonal, harmonic,
Dodecaphonic;
Concerted in effort, symphonic,
Or absolutely simple and singable.
Those old wives' tales, the ballads,
Unfold ancient stories
That stall for time,
Submerge themselves.
Into the same ocean drop the names
Of the great ones whose tunes
Call out to posterity,
Beckon like bells:
Bach to Berg and beyond.
Music has no frontiers,
Being an embraceable art,
And so alongside Stravinsky
Is Elvis intoning the same raw truth
That takes the edge off the emotions.

And you, dear Bob, with your headphones on,
Saturating yourself in Verdi and Rossini,
Are receiving and returning
The message of music
Which is that our species
Can, by listening, survive.

Alan Bold *Music* (for Bob Giddings) (1983)

'I rarely listen to music nowadays, because it doesn't do
to awaken longings that cannot be fulfilled.'

Enoch Powell, in an interview with **John Mortimer**, in *In
Character* (1983)

'I don't like aleatoric music. A piece of art must be
definitely done, and finished. It may be a torso because it
got broken or was not finished; but it was finished in the
artist's fantasy. Every artist must try to find form, and
shape. A chaotic sound is not a piece of art.'

Rafael Kubelik, in an interview with **Gillian
Widdicombe**, in *The Observer* (10 July 1983)

Music of the Spheres

There's music in the sighing of a reed;
There's music in the gushing of a rill;
There's music in all things, if men had ears:
Their earth is but an echo of the spheres.

George Byron *Don Juan*, Canto xv (1819–24)

'There is music wherever there is harmony, order, or
proportion; and thus far we may maintain the music of
the spheres; for those well-ordered motions and regular
paces, though they give no sound to the ear, yet to the
understanding they strike a note most full of harmony.'

Sir Thomas Browne *Religio medici*, Part ii, section 9 (1642)

Musicians

But God has a few of us whom he whispers in the ear;
The rest may reason and welcome: 'tis we
    musicians know.

Robert Browning *Abt Vogler* (1864)

Musorgsky, Modest (1839–81)

'The important thing in this opera [*Boris Godunov*] seems
to be the psychological aspect of the characterization of
the hero, the other figures, and the people, who are not
treated as a mass, a "chorus". There is nothing truer, less

operatic, more affecting in the literature of opera . . . than the "mechanical clock" scene, which synchronizes its tick-tock with the usurper's qualms of conscience. All the other figures are sketched in with like force: the old and venerable monk who in his cell is writing the history of Russia, the drunken mendicant friar, the coarse barmaid, the motherly nurse, the children of the usurper, the sweet and treacherous nobleman, the idiot – all members of *one* people, the Russian. . . .'

Alfred Einstein *Music in the Romantic Era* (1947)

Nationalism

Brahms always claimed to be 'echt deutsch'. It was once brought to his attention that art has 'no fatherland'. He answered: 'That may be true for those who listen. But not for those who write'.

'A nation creates music – the composer only arranges it.'

Mikhail Glinka, quoted in *Theatre Arts* (June 1958)

'The whole music of Western Europe is inconceivable without the ground note of the folk music of the various individual nations: German folk-song and German hymn course no less strongly in Bach's blood than do Chopin's native mazurkas in his. In Berlioz there is a queer mixture of French romance and Italian song; in Schumann, Wagner, Mozart, Verdi, Debussy the national character of their music is unmistakable. Mahler, the Jew, could have wished to avoid hearing the excessive seconds of Eastern European Jewish folk-song that mysteriously surrounded him; he sought a home in German and Czech melodies, but eventually came to rest musically in his ancestral Asiatic homeland.'

Max Brod *Leoš Janáček* (1925)

Nikisch, Arthur (1855–1922)

'I can say that Wagner's *Eroica* in Vienna and then the Ninth at Bayreuth were an absolutely decisive influence, not only on my later grasp of Beethoven, but on my whole understanding of orchestral interpretation. To speak only of the obvious things: Wagner was certainly not what one might describe as a "routine conductor" – his very gestures were music in themselves. I have said before that the conductor's baton-technique – if he is not just an uninspired time-beater – is a language whose mastery enables the listener to penetrate the feelings of the artist, and helps his understanding of the work being played. This was Wagner through and through.'

Arthur Nikisch, quoted in **David Wooldridge** *Conductor's World* (1970)

Noise

'A stench in the ear. Undomesticated music. The chief product and authenticating sign of civilisation.'

Ambrose Bierce *The Devil's Dictionary* (1911)

'Of all noises I think music the least disagreeable.'

Samuel Johnson, quoted in the *Morning Chronicle* (16 Aug 1816)

Oboe

The jolly god in triumph comes;
Sound the trumpets; beat the drums:
   Flush'd with a purple grace
   He shows his honest face;
Now give the hautboys breath; he comes, he comes!
   Bacchus ever fair and young,
   Drinking joys did first ordain;
Bacchus' blessings are a treasure,
Drinking is the soldier's pleasure,
   Sweet is pleasure after pain.

John Dryden *Alexander's Feast* (1697)

'. . . with the tender accents of his oboe.'

Ann Radcliffe *The Mysteries of Udolpho* (1794)

In his early days as a music reporter in Baltimore, H.L. Mencken covered the concerts given by the several Italian bands entertaining the city. In describing one of them he wrote:
   'The only oboist in the band, who had to double in the English horn, was naturally insane, for mental aberration is almost normal among oboists, but he was worse than the common run, for his lunacy took the form of trying to blow the oboe and the English horn at once – a preposterous feat, of no practical use or sense.'

H.L. Mencken *The Tone Art* (1903)

Offenbach, Jacques (1819–80)

'Time signature, 2/4. A non-stop fast oom-pah, oom-pah rhythm in quaver movement, the bass thumping away in crotchets (the "oom"), the harmony flicking the off-beats (the "pah"). The melody, too, keeps up an almost continuous quaver movement, with only short and striking interjections of a few longer notes. Harmony: three chords only, tonic, dominant and subdominant. . . . Phrases in multiples of four bars – no fancy complications. Feminine phrase-endings, the point of these being that at the end of an 8 or 16 bar phrase there is never more than one beat of repose, and often only half a beat. In the fast tempo this gives an effect of breathlessness. . . . Add to this one vital feature: the can-can always goes on for a long time in relation to its own speed. The result is a sensation of breathless, unremitting, mounting energy, with a pounding beat that frequently has the audience clapping and stamping in time to the music.'

Alexander Faris, describing the can-can, the 'Galop infernal' in the bacchanal of the operetta *Orpheus in the Underworld*, in *Jaques Offenbach* (1980)

On 5 October 1880 the actor Léonce, celebrated in comic roles, called at the apartment of his close friend, Offenbach. When the servant answered the door, he asked after his master's health, and was told that Offenbach had died peacefully in his sleep, 'without knowing anything about it'. Léonce commented: 'Aha! He will be very surprised when he finds out!'

'The laughter I hear in Offenbach's music is that of the Empress Charlotte, gone mad.'

François Mauriac, of Offenbach's operetta *La Grande-Duchesse de Gérolstein*

Opera

'Bed is the poor man's opera.'

Italian proverb

'An opera may be allowed to be extravagantly lavish in its decorations, as its only design is to gratify the senses and keep up an indolent attention in the audience.'

Joseph Addison, in *The Spectator* (6 March 1711)

'Whenever I go to an opera, I leave my sense and reason at the door with my half guinea, and deliver myself up to my eyes and my ears.'

Lord Chesterfield, in a letter to his son of 23 Jan 1752

'In 1646 and 1654 Cardinal Mazarin had Italian operas performed by singers specially come from Italy on the boards of the Palais-Royal theatre and the Petit-Bourbon, not far from the Louvre. This new entertainment had been recently invented in Florence, a state then favoured by fortune as well as by nature, and to which we owe the revival of several arts that had lain unknown for centuries, and even the creation of a few. There still remained in France a remnant of ancient barbarism which was opposed to the introduction of these arts.'

Voltaire *The Age of Louis XIV* (1751)

'If a thing isn't worth saying, you sing it.'

Pierre Beaumarchais *The Barber of Seville* (1775)

'Going to the opera, like getting drunk, is a sin that carries its own punishment with it, and that a very severe one.'

Hannah Moore, in a letter to her sister of 1775

'The Opera is a fine thing: the only question is, whether it is not too fine. It is the most fascinating, and at the same time the most tantalising, of all places. It is not the *too little*, but the *too much*, that offends us. Every object is there collected, and displayed in ostentatious profusion, that can strike the senses or dazzle the imagination; music, dancing, painting, poetry, architecture, the blaze of beauty ... and yet one is not satisfied – for the multitude and variety of objects distract the attention, and, by flattering us with a vain show of the highest gratification of every faculty and wish, leave us at last in a state of listlessness, disappointment, and *ennui*. The powers of the mind are exhausted, without being invigorated; our expectations are excited, not satisfied; and we are at some loss to distinguish an excess of irritation from the height of enjoyment. To sit at the Opera for a whole evening is like undergoing the process of animal magnetism for the same length of time. It is an illusion and a mockery, where the mind is made "the fool of the senses" and cheated of itself; where pleasure after pleasure courts us, as in a fairy palace; where the Graces and the Muses, weaving in a gay, fantastic round with one another, still turn from our pursuit; where art, like an enchantress with a thousand faces, still allures our giddy admiration, shifts her mask, and again eludes us. The Opera, in short, proceeds upon a false estimate of taste and morals; it supposes that the capacity for enjoyment may be multiplied with the objects calculated to afford it. It is a species of intellectual prostitution; for we can no more receive pleasure from all our faculties at once than we can be in love with a number of mistresses at the same time.'

William Hazlitt 'Notes of a Journey Through France and Italy' in the *Morning Chronicle* (1825)

'A play representing life in another world, whose inhabitants have no speech but song, no motions but gestures and no postures but attitudes. All acting is simulation, and the word *simulation* is from *simia*, an ape; but in opera the actor takes for his model *Simia audibilis* (or *Pithecanthropus stentor*) – the ape that howls.'

Ambrose Bierce *The Devil's Dictionary* (1911)

'No good opera plot can be sensible, for people do not sing when they are feeling sensible.'

W.H. Auden, quoted in *Time* (29 Dec 1961)

'When it's grand opera in the purest and worst sense of
the nineteenth century tradition, I always find a lot of it
slightly ludicrous. Some of the libretti are beyond me. I
mean, even if the music is a work of genius, who ever
understands *Il Trovatore*?'

André Previn, quoted in **Martin Bookspan** and **Ross
Yockey** *André Previn: a Biography* (1981)

'I think the opera is the proper place for lyric theatre,
rather than the spoken drama. And what I see about
some of those early plays is that they now seem to me to
be libretti *manqués*.'

W.H. Auden, quoted in **Humphrey Carpenter**
W.H. Auden (1981)

Opera on Television

'. . . it was the kind of thing that gives opera a bad name.
Just when the increased use of subtitles is beginning to
give the viewing public a chance of overcoming the one
big stumbling block that lies between them and the
glories of the international operatic repertory, somebody
puts the clock back by giving us Wagner in English. But
what *kind* of English? ''My blood runs cold with nameless
terror'''.

Clive James, on the BBC2 production of *The Flying
Dutchman*, in *The Observer* (27 Feb 1977)

'The settings and costumes recalled the Orson Welles
film of the same name, a cheap rush-job which in turn
recalled Eisenstein. . . . The banquet scene was set in a
cross between an automat and a launderette, with a
plastic pig rotating on a spit. Containing some of Verdi's
finest early music, this is a hard scene to muck up, but
here was proof that it can be done. The final battle was
feeble beyond belief. Banquo's ghost . . . turned up as a
head on a platter – suddenly it's *Salome*! What Macbeth
was doing with a Star of David scratched on his chest I
hesitate to think. But enough.'

Clive James, on Brian Large's BBC2 production of
Macbeth, in *The Observer* (20th Nov 1977)

'. . . in 1976 a thirty one year old French theatre director,
whose sole previous operatic productions were the *Tales
of Hoffmann* and *Il Turco in Italia* created a furore at
Bayreuth by damming the Rhine, caging the woodbird,
putting Fafnir in a garage, setting up steam-engines in
the woods and having Siegfried end up in a dinner-
jacket: the general effect of which was to have staged
Shaw's Fabian account of the *Ring* – political, yes,
Marxist, no. Very quickly the *succès de scandale* turned

into a *succès fou*. Fate saw to it that this was the first *Ring* to be filmed for television, attracting an audience of around a million when it was shown act by act – ratings that Wagner would not have despised. The Chéreau/ Boulez *Ring* confirmed the truism that television has changed once and for all everyone's experience of opera.'

Patrick Carnegy, on the Bayreuth Festival production of the *Ring*, directed by Patrice Chéreau and conducted by Pierre Boulez, shown on BBC2 in 1982, in *The Times Literary Supplement* (26 Aug 1983)

Opera Singers

'A famous young woman, an Italian, was hired by our Comedians to sing on the stage, during so many plays, for which they gave her £500; which part by her voice alone at the end of three scenes she performed with such modesty and grace, and above all, with such skill, that there was never any who did anything comparable with their voices. She was to go home to the court of the King of Prussia, and I believe carried with her out of this vain nation above £1,000, everybody covetting to hear her at their private houses.'

John Evelyn *Diary*, entry for Feb 1703

Ophicleide

The consoling powers of music sometimes fail. This is well testified in the history of one of George Bernard Shaw's relatives:

'One uncle, deciding to reform, gave up drinking and smoking at one blow and intemperately tooted the ophicleide instead. This not giving him sufficient solace, he married. Even that did not seem to give him the happiness he thought he deserved, so he bought a pair of opera-glasses and a Bible. When he tired of reading the Bible, he would turn the opera-glasses on the girls swimming at Dalkey Beach. This "reformed" man finally committed suicide. . . .'

Frank Harris *Bernard Shaw – An Unauthorised Biography Based on Firsthand Information* (1931)

Oratorio

'Nothing can be more disgusting than oratorio. How absurd, to see five hundred people fiddling like madmen about the Israelites in the Red Sea!'

Sydney Smith, in a letter to Lady Holland of 1 Oct 1823

Orchestra

One of the greatest influences on the creation of the modern symphony orchestra was the celebrated Mannheim court orchestra of the mid-18th century, particularly while it was under the direction of Johann Stamitz, from 1741 to 1757. Dr Charles Burney, the English musical scholar and diarist, visited Mannheim in 1772 and left a very fine account of this virtuoso orchestra. Schwetzingen, a village outside Mannheim, was apparently inhabited solely by musicians.

'Here it was a violinist who was practising; in the next house, a flautist; there an oboe; a bassoon; a clarionett; a 'cello; or a concert of several instruments combined. The music seemed the principal object in life . . . [the orchestra] contained, by itself, perhaps more distinguished virtuosi and composers than any other in Europe; it was an army of generals. . . . It was here that Stamitz, for the first time, ventured to cross the boundaries of the ordinary operatic overtures, which until then had merely served to challenge attention and impose silence. . . . This brilliant and ingenious musician created the modern symphonic style by the addition of the majestic effects of light and shade which he used to enrich it. First of all the various effects were tested which could be produced by the combination of notes and tones; then a practical understanding of the *crescendo* and *diminuendo* was acquired in the orchestra; and the *piano*, which until then had been employed only as synonymous with echo, became, with the *forte*, an abundant source of colours which have their gamut of shades in music just as red and blue have in painting.'

Charles Burney *A General History of Music* (1776)

In days of old, when Englishmen were men,
Their music, like themselves, was grave and plain;
The manly trumpets, and the simple reed,
Alike with citizen and simple swain agreed.
But now, since Britons are become polite,
Since few can read, and fewer still can write;
Since South-Sea schemes have so enriched the land,
That footmen 'gainst their lords for boroughs stand;
Since masquerades and operas made their entry,
And Heydegger reign'd guardian of our gentry;
A hundred various instruments combine,
And foreign songsters in the concert join;
The Gallic horn, whose winding tube in vain
Pretends to emulate the trumpet's strain;
The shrill-toned fiddle and the warbling flute,
The grave bassoon, deep brass, and tinkling lute,
All league, melodious nonsense to dispense,
And give us sound, and show, instead of sense.

James Miller (1706–44) *Humours of Oxford* (1730)

Orchestral Players

A squeak's heard in the orchestra,
   The leader draws across
The intestines of the agile cat
   The tail of the noble hoss.
George T. Lanigan (1845–86) *The Amateur Orlando*

See to their desks Apollo's sons repair,
Swift rides the rosin o'er the horse's hair!
In unison their various tones to tune,
Murmurs the hautboy, growls the hoarse bassoon;
In soft vibration sighs the whispering lute,
Tang goes the harpsichord, too-too the flute,
Brays the loud trumpet, squeaks the fiddle sharp,
Winds the French horn, and twangs the tingling harp;
Till, like great Jove, the leader, figuring in,
Attunes to order the chaotic din.
Horace and **James Smith** *Rejected Addresses – The Theatre*
(1812)

'How do orchestras differ, over the world, I mean?'
'That's a question you either can't answer or you could
write a book about it. Superficially you could say the
Germans are the most obedient, and the richest. Americans call you by your Christian name at the first
rehearsal. English musicians must be the hardest
worked, worst paid collection of players in the world. In
America they're on a salary, in England they get paid by
the work they do. That's why they have to sandwich
beer commercials and film sessions in between Schubert
symphonies.'
André Previn, in an interview with **John Mortimer**, in
The Sunday Times (20 March 1983)

Organ

'Hence from their resounding prison the docile winds are
loosed, and repay a melody for their liberty received.'
Jean Baptist de Santeul (1630–97) *Inscription on an Organ*

There let the pealing organ blow,
To the full-voiced choir below,
In service high, and anthems clear,
As may with sweetness, through mine ear,
Dissolve me into ecstasies,
And bring all Heav'n before mine eyes.
John Milton *Il penseroso* (1632)

But O! what art can teach,
What human voice can reach,
The sacred organ's praise?
Notes inspiring holy love,
Notes that wing their heavenly ways
To mend the choirs above.
John Dryden *A Song for St. Cecilia's Day* (1687)

Orpheus

By the streams that ever flow,
By the fragrant winds that blow
  O'er th'Elysian flow'rs;
By those happy souls who dwell
In yellow meads of Asphodel,
  Or Amaranthine bowers;
By the heroes' armed shades,
Glittering thro' the gloomy glades;
By the youths that dy'd for love,
Wand'ring in the myrtle grove,
Restore, restore Eurydice to life:
Oh take the husband, or return the wife!
  He sung, and hell consented
    To hear the Poet's prayer;
  Stern Proserpine relented,
    And gave him back the fair.
    Thus song could prevail
    O'er death, and o'er hell,
A conquest how hard and how glorious?
  Tho' fate had fast bound her
  With Styx nine times round her,
Yet music and love were victorious.
But soon, too soon, the lover turns his eyes;
Again she falls, again she dies, she dies!
How wilt thou now the fatal sisters move?
No crime was thine, if 'tis no crime to love.
  Now under hanging mountains,
  Beside the falls of fountains,
    Or where Hebrus wanders,
  Rolling in Maeanders,
    All alone,
    Unheard, unknown,
    He makes his moan;
    And calls her ghost,
For ever, ever, ever lost!
Now with Furies surrounded,
Despairing, confounded,
He trembles, he glows,
Amidst Rhodope's snows:
See, wild as the winds, o'er the desert he flies;
Hark! Haemus resounds with the Bacchanals cries –
  Ah see, he dies!
Yet ev'n in death Eurydice he sung,
Eurydice still trembled on his tongue,
  Eurydice the woods,
  Eurydice the floods,
Eurydice the rocks, and hollow mountains rung.
  Music the fiercest grief can charm,
  And fate's severest rage disarm:
  Music can soften pain to ease,
  And make despair and madness please:
  Our joys below it can improve,
  And antedate the bliss above.
  This the divine Cecilia found,

And to her Maker's praise confin'd the sound.
When the full organ joins the tuneful choir,
   Th' immortal pow'rs incline their ear;
Borne on the swelling notes our souls aspire,
While solemn airs improve the sacred fire;
   And Angels lean from heav'n to hear.
Of Orpheus now no more let Poets tell,
To bright Cecilia greater pow'r is giv'n;
   His numbers rais'd a shade from hell,
   Hers lift the soul to heav'n.

Alexander Pope *An Ode for Music on St Cecilia's Day* (1708)

Orpheus with his lute made trees,
And the mountain tops that freeze,
Bow themselves when he did sing;
To his music plants and flowers
Ever sprung, as sun and showers
There had made a lasting spring.

Everything that heard him play,
Even the billows of the sea,
Hung their heads and then lay by.
In sweet music is such art,
Killing care and grief of heart
Fall asleep or hearing die.

William Shakespeare *Henry VIII*, Act III, scene i (1613)

When Orpheus strikes the trembling lyre,
The streams stand still, the stones admire;
The listening savages advance,
The wolf and lamb around him trip,
The bears in awkward measures leap,
And tigers mingle in the dance:
The moving woods attended as he played,
And Rhodophe was left without a shade.

Joseph Addison *Song for St Cecilia's Day* (1712)

O'Sullivan, John (1878–1955)

John O'Sullivan was a remarkable Irish–French tenor,
born in Cork, who studied in Paris. His voice was of
considerable range, strong tone and great flexibility. He
sang leading roles at the Opéra in Paris and in Italy and
Covent Garden. It was said that when he sang 'Esultate!
L'orgoglio musulmano sepolto é in mar; nostra e del ciel
é gloria' at Covent Garden, he could be heard in the
street outside. His top notes had a trumpet-like ringing
quality which many believe have never been matched.
He was ideally suited to Verdi's heroic roles and excelled
in the part of Raoul in Meyerbeer's *Les Huguenots*.
O'Sullivan was a friend of James Joyce, who felt that the
great Irish singer had not really had the press he
deserved. Joyce wrote this punning appreciation of him:

'Just out of kerryosity howlike is a Sullivan? It has the fortefaccia of a Markus Brutas, the wingthud of a spreadeagle, the body uniformed of a metropoliceman with brass feet of a collared grand. It cresces up in Aquilone but diminuends austrowards. It was last seen and heard of by some macgillicuddies above a lonely valley of their reeks, duskening the grey light as it flew, its cry echechohooing among the anfractuosities: *pour la dernière fois*. The black-bulled ones, stampeding, drew in their horns, all appailed and much upset, which explaints the guttermilk on their overcoats.'

James Joyce 'From a Banned Writer to a Banned Singer', in the *New Statesman* (1932) [Joyce's novel *Ulysses* had recently been banned in the USA]

Some of the references need explanation: O'Sullivan comes from Kerry ('kerryosity') where there are mountains called Mcgillicuddy's Reeks. He is tall and well built, big enough to be a policeman. His feet are large – they are compared to the feet of a Collard grand. He is big in voice as well. Aquilone refers to the North wind, and the Auster is the South wind – Joyce punningly implies here that O'Sullivan has an aquiline nose and his voice could swell into a crescendo ('it cresces up') of swelling sound, and then decline into sweetness and softness like a gentle wind. The quote: 'pour la dernière fois' is a reference to Rossini's *William Tell* and the scene where Arnold (one of O'Sullivan's finest roles) makes his last visit to his home – O'Sullivan had recently made his last visit to his home in Ireland.

Paderewski, Ignacy Jan
(1860–1941)

'By the time I reached Paderewski's concert on Tuesday last week, his concerto was over, the audience in wild enthusiasm, and the pianoforte a wreck. Regarded as an immensely spirited young harmonious blacksmith, who puts a concerto on the piano as upon an anvil, and hammers it out with an exuberant enjoyment of the swing and strength of the proceeding, Paderewski is at least exhilarating; and his hammer-play is not without variety, some of it being feathery, if not delicate. But his touch, light or heavy, is the touch that hurts; and the glory of his playing is the glory that attends murder on a large scale when impetuously done. Besides, the piano is not an instrument upon which you can safely let yourself go in this fashion.'

George Bernard Shaw *Music in London 1890–94* (1932), entry for 18 June 1890

Patti, Adelina (1843–1919)

At a production of Gounod's *Roméo et Juliette* at the Opéra in Paris an audience was once treated to a real-life love scene, when during the balcony scene in Act II the leading tenor and the prima donna genuinely and lovingly embraced, implanting no less than 29 real kisses on each other's lips. The lovers were Ernest Nicolini (1834–98) and Adelina Patti (1843–1919). At the time Patti was married to the Marquise de Caux, but that this marriage was not to last much longer and that the Romeo and Juliet on stage were deeply in love was made very plain to an appreciative audience: 'O nuit divine', sang Nicolini, and Patti replied 'Ah! je te l'ai dit, je t'adore!'

Herman Klein *The Reign of Patti* (1920)

'Her flawless technique and even *timbre* throughout her compass were proof of the perfection of her training; no signs of headiness in the top notes, nor 'mouthiness' in the medium, and certainly no over-brightness or vulgarity in her chest tones. . . . I believe she earned £35,000 a year by her singing. She deserved every penny of it.'

Sir Henry Wood *My Life of Music* (1938)

'On Saturday afternoon the Albert Hall was filled by the attraction of our still adored Patti, now the most accomplished of mezzo-sopranos. It always amuses me to see that vast audience from the squares and villas listening with moist eyes whilst the opulent lady from the celebrated Welsh castle fervently sings: Oh give me my lowly thatched cottage again. The concert was a huge success: there were bouquets, raptures, effusions, kissings of children, graceful sharings of the applause with obbligato players – in short, the usual exhibition of the British bourgeoisie in the part of Bottom and the prima donna in the part of Titania.'

George Bernard Shaw *Music in London 1890–94* (1932)

Pauses

'The notes I handle no better than many pianists. But the pauses between the notes – ah – that is where the art resides.'

Artur Schnabel, quoted in the *Chicago Daily News* (11 June 1958)

Piano

'Some new neighbours, that came a month or two ago, brought with them an accumulation of all the things to be guarded against in a London neighbourhood, viz., a pianoforte, a lap-dog and a parrot.'

Jane Welsh Carlyle, in a letter to Mrs Carlyle of 6 May 1839

'Hints to those who have pianofortes: Keep your piano free from dust, and do not allow needles, pins, or bread to be placed upon it, especially if the key-board is exposed, as such articles are apt to get inside and produce a jarring or whizzing sound.'

Enquire Within upon Everything (1860)

'There is always a piano in an hotel drawing room, on which, of course, some one of the forlorn ladies is employed. I do not suppose that these pianos are in fact, as a rule, louder and harsher, more violent and less musical, than other instruments of the kind. They seem to be so, but that, I take it, arises from the exceptional mental depression of those who have to listen to them.'

Anthony Trollope *North America* (1862)

'A parlour utensil for subduing the impenitent visitor. It is operated by depressing the keys of the machine and the spirits of the audience.'

Ambrose Bierce *The Devil's Dictionary* (1911)

'There is no sort of doubt that the pianoforte must succumb sooner or later to the overwhelming objection that you can hear it next door. In an age of general insensibility to music this does not matter; the ordinary citizen today, who regards pianoforte playing as a mere noise, may drop an oath or two when the young lady at the other side of the party-wall begins practising; but he soon gets used to it as he gets used to passing trains, factory hooters, fog signals, and wheel traffic. Make a musician of him, however, and his tolerance will vanish. I live, when I am at home, in a London square which is in a state of transition from the Russell Square private house stage to the Soho or Golden Square stage of letting for all sorts of purposes. There are a couple of clubs, with "bars" and social musical evenings, not unrelieved by occasional clog dances audible a quarter of a mile off. There is a residence for the staff of a monster emporium which employs several talented tenors behind its counters. There is a volunteer headquarters in which the band practises on the first floors whilst the combatants train themselves for the thousand yards range by shooting through Morris tubes in the area. Yet I have sat at work on a summer evening with every window in the square open and all these resources in full blast, and found myself less disturbed than I have been by a single private pianoforte, of the sort that the British householder thinks "brilliant", played by a female with no music in her whole composition, simply getting up an "accomplishment" either to satisfy her own vanity or to obey the orders of her misguided mother. Now if such females had spinets to play on instead of pianos, I should probably not hear them.'

George Bernard Shaw *Music in London 1890–94* (1932), entry for 11 Jan 1893

Softly, in the dusk, a woman is singing to me;
Taking me back down the vista of years, till I see
A child sitting under the piano, in the boom of the
    tingling strings
And pressing the small, poised feet of a mother who
    smiles as she sings.

In spite of myself, the insidious mastery of song
Betrays me back, till the heart of me weeps to belong
To the old Sunday evenings at home, with
    winter outside
And hymns in the cosy parlour, the tinkling piano
    our guide.

So now it is vain for the singer to burst into clamour
With the great black piano appassionato. The glamour
Of childish days is upon me, my manhood is cast
Down in the flood of remembrance, I weep like a child
    for the past.

D.H. Lawrence *Piano* (1918)

'The human soul needs actual beauty even more than bread. The middle classes jeer at the colliers for buying pianos – but what is the piano, often as not, but a blind reaching out for beauty. To the woman it is a possession and a piece of furniture and something to feel superior about. But to see the elderly colliers trying to learn to play, see them listening with queer alert faces to their daughter's execution of "The Maiden's Prayer", and you will see a blind, unsatisfied craving for beauty. It is far more deep in the men than the women. The women want show. The men want beauty, and still want it.'

D.H. Lawrence 'Nottingham and the Mining Countryside', in *New Adelphi* (June–Aug 1930)

Previn, André (born 1929)

'I'm really lucky to be so crazy about music, so enamoured by the sound of it. . . .I feel so sorry for critics who get dulled down to the point where they're nothing more than reacting machines no longer pleased to hear Brahms Four. . . . I'm still childish enough in my musical attitudes that I'd love to hear the Brahms Fourth Symphony played by the Used Car Dealers Orchestra of

Akron, Ohio. I wouldn't expect to hear it played to perfection, but I'd still love to hear it.'

André Previn, quoted in **Martin Bookspan** and **Ross Yockey** *André Previn: a Biography* (1981)

Prokofiev, Sergey (1891–1953)

'Prokofiev was lucky from childhood on ... he always had money and success.... Chekhov once said: "The Russian writer lives in a drainpipe, eats woodlice, and sleeps with washerwomen". In that sense, Prokofiev was never a Russian.... For some fifteen years Prokofiev sat between two stools – in the West he was considered a Soviet and in Russia they welcomed him as a Western guest.'

Dmitri Shostakovich *Testimony: the Memoirs of Dmitri Shostakovich* (1979)

'Prokofiev looked younger than his years thanks to the boyish expression on his face which he kept all his life. Rather tall, strongly build, a little shy and gauche, he had the features of a white negro, a flat nose and large red lips. He had white, almost invisible eyebrows and light hair. His complexion was so delicate that he blushed at the slightest provocation.... Prokofiev played me his works in progress; he laughingly admitted that he had picked up two sonatas written for his exams in the conservatory and was now modernizing them.... He was also busy composing his third concerto and some short pieces he called *Visions fugitives*; he played a few of them for me. They sounded strange but had a refreshing novel quality which attracted me right away....'

Artur Rubinstein *My Many Years* (1980)

Puccini, Giacomo (1858–1924)

'Puccini, returning from Turin, arrived in Milan. It was 19 March 1893.... Puccini went for a stroll in the Galleria, where he naturally ran into some acquaintances. Among them was Ruggero Leoncavallo, whom Puccini had known for several years.... Puccini mentioned to his colleague that he was already at work on his next opera. It was going to be *La bohème*....Leoncavallo was astonished and indignant; he revealed that he was also working on a *Bohème* opera....'

Leoncavallo had recently previously offered Puccini a libretto based on Murger's *Scènes de la vie bohème* but Puccini had rejected it. Consequently, Leoncavallo decided to set the work himself. He published a letter in a newspaper saying that he had been working on a *Bohème* opera for some months, attempting to claim prior rights. Puccini's answer was simple: let Leoncavallo write his version and he would write his own – the public would judge between them.

On 25 April 1926 Puccini's last opera, *Turandot*, was first performed at La Scala, Milan. He had not lived to complete it and the final scenes were finished by the composer Franco Alfano (1875–1954). The completed version was not played at that extraordinary première. When he reached the end of Liù's death-scene, Toscanini laid down his baton and said: 'The opera ends here, because at this point the Maestro died. Death was stronger than art.' Weaver suggests there is more weight in Toscanini's words: 'The opera ends here. Toscanini might have been speaking not just of Puccini's last work but of Italian opera in general. . . . Puccini left no Crown Prince. With him, the glorious line, Rossini, Bellini, Donizetti, Verdi, came to a glorious conclusion.'

William Weaver *The Golden Century of Italian Opera from Rossini to Puccini* (1980)

'Those people who love opera owe a debt of gratitude, greater than they may realize, to Giacomo Puccini. . . . His world is the world of strong theatre, violent melodrama, easy pathos. He was one of those artists . . . who discover early in their careers just what they are best fitted to do, and are satisfied to stick to that. . . . We ought surely to be thankful that, instead of producing travesties of Shakespeare and Goethe, Puccini was content to embellish Sardou and transfigure David Belasco. To such theatrical material he brought a power (unique, it seems, among his contemporaries and successors) of expressing dramatic emotion in terms of melody. . . . Puccini's music is not profound, but it transmits abundant impressions of charm, tenderness, passion, pathos: in short, of humanity. . . .'

Edward Sackville-West and **Desmond Shawe-Taylor** *The Record Guide* (1951)

Shostakovich: 'What do you think of Puccini?'
Benjamin Britten: 'I think his operas are dreadful.'
Shostakovich: 'No, Ben, you are wrong. He wrote marvellous operas, but dreadful music.'

Quoted in *The Tongs and the Bones: the Memoirs of Lord Harewood* (1981)

Purcell, Henry (1659–95)

'He was so superior to all his predecessors, that his compositions seemed to speak a new language; yet, however, different from that to which the public had been long accustomed, it was universally understood. His songs seem to contain whatever the ear could then wish, or heart could feel.'

Charles Burney *A General History of Music* (1776)

'To listen is to share an experience, to catch some of his glancing fire and to have a part of his aching regret. He was a man of changing moods and sympathies, ready to boast, to worship, to sigh and to lament. He could bid the trumpets to sound for majesty, or seeking flight from love's sickness find the fever in himself.'

Sir Jack Westrup *Purcell* (1937)

Puritanism

'This sort of music warms the passions, and unlocks the fancy, and makes it open to pleasure, like a flower to the sun.... When the music is soft, exquisite and airy, 'tis dangerous and ensnaring.'

Jeremy Collier *A Short View of the Immorality and Profanity of the English Stage* (1698)

'I say of music as Plato, Aristotle, Galen and many others have said of it: that it is very ill for young heads, for a certain kind of nice, smooth sweetness in alluring the auditory to niceness, effeminacy, pusillanimity, and loathesomeness of life ... and made apt to all wantonness and sin. And therefore writers affirm Sappho to have been expert in music, and therefore whorish.'

Philip Stubbes *The Anatomy of Abuses* (1583)

Rakhmaninov, Sergey (1873–1943)

'He was superlative when he played his own music. A performance of his concertos would make you believe that they were the greatest masterpieces ever written, while when played by other pianists, even at their best, they became clearly what they were: brilliantly written pieces with their Oriental langour which have retained a great hold on the public. But when he played the music of other composers, he impressed me by the novelty and the originality of his conceptions. When he played a Schumann or a Chopin, even if it was contrary to my own feelings, he could convince me by the sheer impact of his personality. He was the most fascinating pianist of them all since Busoni. He had the secret of the golden, living tone which comes from the heart.'

Artur Rubinstein *My Many Years* (1980)

Ravel, Maurice (1875–1937)

'I had a terrible nightmare last night. Ravel's *Bolero* all night long, getting louder and louder, more and more instruments joining in – a huge, huge orchestra – the sound was deafening, my ears were bursting with the sound – and it never modulated to its cadence.... It was relentless, it was going to go on and on and on.'

Pekka Salamaa, comment to the author

Recorded Music

'The gramophone is increasingly assuming a musical role as fundamental as the printed score. Since the publication of the first edition of *The Penguin Stereo Guide* the catalogue has continued to expand at a remarkable pace.... The striking thing about this vast expansion of the recorded repertoire ... is the discovery by the ordinary music lover of areas of music hitherto the exclusive province of the scholar.... The establishment of the box-album format for issuing complete series emphasizes the parallel between printed and recorded music, and a survey of the recorded repertoire, such as undertaken by this book, increasingly becomes an appraisal of the overall achievement of our Western musical culture. Moreover the recorded examples of this culture are readily available to everyone at a cost which continues to defy inflation. It is still possible to buy a major recording for little more than the price of a concert ticket, and in the field of opera this comparison frequently brings a balance of reward distinctly in favour of the record.

The arrival of the tape cassette has finally taken the ritual out of reproduction.'

Edward Greenfield , **Robert Layton** and **Ivan March**
Preface to *The Penguin Stereo Record Guide* (2nd edn, 1979)

Recorder

Re-enter the Players, with recorders
Hamlet: O, the recorders! Let me see one. To withdraw you – why do you go about to recover the wind of me, as if you would drive me into a toil?
Guildenstern: O my lord, if my duty be too bold, my love is too unmannerly.
Hamlet: I do not well understand that. Will you play upon this pipe?
Guildenstern: My lord, I cannot.
Hamlet: I pray you.
Guildenstern: Believe me, I cannot.
Hamlet: I do beseech you.
Guildenstern: I know no touch of it, my lord.

Hamlet: It is as easy as lying: govern these ventages with your fingers and thumb, give it breath with your mouth, and it will discourse most eloquent music. Look you, these are the stops.

Guildenstern: But these cannot I command to any utterance of harmony; I have not the skill.

Hamlet: Why, look you now, how unworthy a thing you make of me! You would play upon me; you would seem to know my stops; you would pluck out the heart of my mystery; you would sound me from my lowest note to the top of my compass; and there is much music, excellent voice, in this little organ, yet cannot you make it speak. 'Sblood, do you think I am easier to be play'd on than a pipe? Call me what instrument you will, though you can fret me, yet you cannot play upon me.

William Shakespeare *Hamlet*, Act III, scene ii (1600)

Lysander: He has rid his prologue like a rough colt; he knows not the stop. A good moral my lord: it is not enough to speak, but to speak true.

Hippolyta: Indeed he hath play'd on this prologue like a child on a recorder – a sound, but not in government.

William Shakespeare *A Midsummer Night's Dream*, Act V, scene i (1595)

Anon they move
In perfect phalanx to the Dorian mood
Of flutes and soft recorders.

John Milton *Paradise Lost*, Book I, line 549 (1667)

Rehearsals

'Already too loud!'

Bruno Walter, at his first rehearsal with an American orchestra, on seeing the players reaching for their instruments

'After I die, I shall return to earth as a gatekeeper of a bordello and I won't let any of you – not a one of you – enter!'

Arturo Toscanini, at a rehearsal with the NBC Symphony Orchestra; quoted in **Howard Taubman** *The Maestro: the Life of Arturo Toscanini* (1951)

At a rehearsal of Wagner's *Tristan und Isolde* Sir Thomas Beecham considered that the English tenor Walter Widdop was not singing his role with sufficient dignity. He said:

'Walter, you are singing divinely. But really, you must carry yourself with more dignity, more pride of carriage. Don't you know who Tristan is supposed to be?' Walter Widdop answered: ''E's only a sailor, isn't he?' Beecham was speechless.

Quoted in **Neville Cardus** *Sir Thomas Beecham* (1961)

'Ladies and gentlemen, if you will make a point of singing *All we, like sheep, have gone astray* with a little less satisfaction, we shall meet the aesthetic as well as the theological requirements.'

Sir Thomas Beecham, during a rehearsal of Handel's *Messiah*; quoted in *Liverpool Echo and Evening Express* (8 March 1961)

'At a rehearsal I let the orchestra play as they like. At the concert I make them play as *I* like.'

Sir Thomas Beecham, quoted in **Neville Cardus** *Sir Thomas Beecham* (1961)

Romanticism

'When Beethoven died in 1827 music already found itself in the midst of an intellectual movement that decided the art of the whole of the 19th. century ... the Romantic movement. The idea of Romanticism embraces such an enormous variety of elements ... that it is useless to attempt to reduce it to any simple formula.... There had been romanticism in music long before there were romantic composers.... What now happened was not so much a discovery as the choice of a new angle of vision. The spirit of the age regarded the things of art exclusively in a romantic light, and saw in them all only the dazzling enchantments of sympathetic colours.

Thus almost the whole of Beethoven came to be hailed as romantic. The prodigious power of his symphonic works seemed a fulfilment of the oracular saying of the 18th. century poet Wackenroder to the effect that instrumental music was the one true art, a heaven that was to be gained by the renunciation of reality.'

Alfred Einstein *A Short History of Music* (1936)

Rossini, Gioachino (1792–1868)

'I was born for *opera buffa*, as well Thou knowest. Little skill, a little heart, and that is all. So be Thou blessed and admit me to Paradise.'

Gioachino Rossini, on the score of his *Petite messe solennelle* (1864)

The aria given to the hero for his first appearance in Rossini's *Tancredi*, 'Tu che accendi.... Di tanti palpiti', was composed under extraordinary circumstances. The role was to be sung at the première in Venice in February 1813 by Signora Adelaide Malanotte, an outstanding beauty and fine singer of a somewhat haughty temperament (she had aristocratic connections). On the day of the première she let it be known in no uncertain manner that she disapproved of her entrance aria. At the last minute Rossini was forced to compose another. He walked back to his lodging in despair. How could one, in such circumstances, compose an aria suitable to express the happiness of two lovers meeting again after long separation? As Stendhal relates, the origins are gastric as much as poetic. In Venice it was called the *aria dei risi*, the 'rice aria'. In Lombardy it is the custom that every dinner begins with a dish of rice:

'. . . and since rice is eaten for preference very much under cooked, four minutes precisely before the course is due, the chef invariably sends a minion with this momentous query: *bisogna mettere i risi?* On that famous evening when Rossini . . . walked slowly back to his lodgings, the *cameriere* asked the usual question; the rice was set to cook; and before it was ready Rossini had completed his aria.'

In discussing the physical impact of music on the human system, Stendhal recounts the evidence of Dr Cotugno, the most distinguished physician in Naples, who testified that many young women died of excitement brought on while enjoying Rossini's *Mosè in Egitto*:

'I could quote you more than forty cases of brain-fever or of violent nervous convulsions among young ladies with an over-ardent passion for music, brought on exclusively by the Jews' Prayer in the third act, with its extraordinary change of key!'

Stendhal *Life of Rossini* (1824)

'Rossini wrote the first and last acts of *William Tell*. God wrote the second act.'

Gaetano Donizetti

'The whole world hurrahed Rossini for his melodies; Rossini, who so admirably knew how to make the employment of these melodies a special art. All organizing of form he left upon one side; the simplest, barrenest, and most transparent that came to hand he filled with all the logical contents it had ever needed – with narcotizing melody. Entirely unconcerned for form, just because he left it altogether undisturbed, he turned his whole genius to the invention of the most amusing hocus-pocus for execution within those forms.'

Richard Wagner *'Opera and Drama'*, in *Richard Wagner's Prose Works*, translated and edited by **William Ashton Ellis 2** (1893)

'Mozart minus the brains.'

Clive James, on *The Barber of Seville*, in *The Observer* (28 Nov 1976)

Rubinstein, Artur (1887–1982)

'The horrible thing in our life is that we must be for the public at least, for their money, perfect at 8.30, not tomorrow morning. I couldn't say to the public, "Well, look here, I'm not now in the mood. I'm a little bit tired. Come back in about two hours or tomorrow morning". So, we must face it. Sometimes we have a headache, we receive a telegram, we have bad news. Suddenly you feel something in your arm or a pain or something. They don't care. And if you tell them that something is wrong, you can play like God Almighty, they will always say: "Poor fellow, one heard that he was sick with a pain or something".'

Artur Rubinstein, in a television interview with David Frost; in **David Frost** *The Americans* (1971)

Sackbut

The trumpets, sackbuts, psalteries, and fifes,
Tabors and cymbals, and the shouting Romans,
Make the sun dance.

William Shakespeare *Coriolanus*, Act V, Scene iv (1607)

see also Trombone

Saint-Saëns, Camille (1835–1921)

'he was not in the least sentimental. I remember an evening in Brussels, in which several of us accompanied him from the hotel to the theatre where the fiftieth performance of his *Samson and Delilah* was to be given as a gala performance. We were all in a festive mood, but Saint-Saëns begged us to excuse him for a moment. When he last passed through Brussels he had left an old hat to be done over. He wished to fetch it now before the hatter shut his shop.'

Ferruccio Busoni *The Essence of Music and other Papers* (1957)

'If he'd been making shell-cases during the war it might have been better for music.'

Maurice Ravel

Sargent, Sir Malcolm (1895–1967)

'He is the greatest choirmaster we have ever produced. Choir conducting is one of the most difficult arts. Myself I can only bring it off occasionally – sometimes in the last act of *Die Meistersinger*, for example. But Malcolm always does it. He makes the b———s sing like blazes!'

Sir Thomas Beecham, in a birthday tribute reported by Lord Boothby on BBC television's *Sargent at Seventy*, 22 April 1965

Satie, Erik (1866–1925)

'Few animals benefit from human instruction. The dog, the mule, the horse, the donkey, the parrot and a few others are the only animals to receive a semblance of education. And yet, can you call it education? Compare this instruction if you please, to that given the young human undergraduate by the universities, and you will see it is worthless, it can neither broaden the knowledge nor facilitate the learning which the animal might have acquired through his own labours, by his own devotion. But musically? Horses have learned to dance; spiders have remained under a piano throughout an entire concert. . . . So what? So nothing. Now and then we are told about the musicality of the starling, the melodic memory of the crow, the harmonic ingenuity of the owl who accompanies himself by tapping his stomach – a purely artificial contrivance and polyphonically meagre.

As for the perennially cited nightingale, his musical knowledge makes his most ignorant auditors shrug. Not only is his voice not placed, but he shows absolutely no knowledge of clefs, tonality, modality or measure. Perhaps he is gifted? Possibly, almost certainly. But it can be stated flatly that his artistic culture does not equal his gifts, and that the voice of which he is so inordinately proud, is nothing but an inferior useless instrument.'

Erik Satie 'Intelligence and Musicality Among the Animals' in *La Revue S.I.M.*, Vol 10, (1914)

Saxophone

In his novel *Brave New World*, Huxley pounces on the inviting half-pun in the saxophone's name – and features a group of these woodwind instruments in the Westminster Abbey Cabaret, where one can cavort to the music of Calvin Stopes and his Sixteen Sexophonists, London's Finest Scent and Colour Organ and All the Latest Synthetic Music. The air is hot and almost breathless with the fragrance of ambergris and sandalwood. The colour organ seems to offer something between a disco light-show and a laser concert. The 16 sexophonists, when readers first meet them, are playing an old favourite, entitled, 'There ain't no Bottle in all the world like that dear little Bottle of mine'. 400 couples are dancing:

'The sexophones wailed like melodious cats under the moon, moaned in the alto and tenor registers as though the little death were upon them. Rich with a wealth of harmonics, their tremulous chorus mounted towards a climax, louder and ever louder ... the conductor let loose the final shattering note of ether music and blew the sixteen merely human blowers clean out of existence. Thunder in A flat major ... then ... there followed a gradual deturgescence, a *diminuendo* sliding gradually, through quarter tones, down, down to a faintly whispered dominant chord that lingered on.'

Aldous Huxley *Brave New World* (1932)

Casals has described the problems he had getting players for the high trumpet parts in Bach orchestral works during the Prades festivals. On one occasion the player he had engaged could not play the Brandenburg Concerto no. 2 at the tempo Casals wanted, the one he believed would keep the music alive. The trumpeter played wrong notes and in the end admitted he simply could not go on in this way. An unusual alternative was proposed:

'It was suggested that we could try the soprano saxophone which, well played, gave an excellent result. There were some purists who, when they learned of the change, were scandalized.... I am not inclined to use the trumpet in these works because it has to be played too much in the higher register. The soprano saxophone, if it is well played, can take its place with advantage.'

Pablo Casals, in **J.M.A. Corredor** *Conversations with Casals* (1956)

Schoenberg, Arnold (1874–1951)

'Schönberg is too melodious for me, too sweet.'

Bertolt Brecht, quoted in *Brecht as they Knew him*, edited by **Hubert Witt** (1974)

In January 1914 Schoenberg wrote a letter to the *Daily Telegraph*, addressed to the members of the Queen's Hall Orchestra, in appreciation of their performances of his music in London. The last sentence of the letter, in view of the fact that it was published barely six months before the outbreak of the Great War, seems amazingly prescient:

'DEAR SIRS,

I wish to tell you that you have given me great pleasure. By that I mean not only the numerous manifestations of sympathy with which you have honoured me, and which gave me such a pleasant feeling at the rehearsals, but also the careful way with which you played in my rehearsals and the performances.

Such achievements are in absolute harmony with your

artistic qualities. These are such as appeal mostly to the artist who can look ahead. I mean your present mastership in your performances and the unexcelled qualities of your "ensemble", the precision, beauty of sound, and noble taste and careful thoroughness of every detail, which are the merit of every single one of you and the success of all of you together. I must tell you that on the Continent, as far as my knowledge goes, there are only at the most two orchestras which would be compared with you – the Amsterdam Orchestra and the Viennese Philharmonic.

I must say it was the first time since Gustav Mahler that I heard such music played again as a musician of culture demands. I presume that this letter will be published, and that is the reason I mention this fact, so that it should be taken note of by some of our German orchestras, who have too much false pride to learn what is expected of them at the present time.

They may learn what is required of them by modern composers, and they may learn how easily an artistic predominance is lost if untiring energy and a most essential sense of duty are not constantly at work, as well as a renewal of technical knowledge.

It was a great pleasure to me to find your orchestra a confirmation of the fact that the last technical acquirements of the instrumental soloists in concerts, not only in playing soli, but also in full orchestra, can be made use of. This I have long known, it is true, but have not heard anything about it for a long time. That it is possible to play in tune the quickest movements distinctly, clearly, and the same in *pianissimo*; that difficult parts can also be rendered purely and sonorously; that – but need I tell you all I understand, but which to many a famous orchestra appears to be an unjust demand? That is indeed the praise I have for you. One must always aim higher, as you know: therefore, in conclusion I say once more that I experienced a great pleasure, which has only been troubled by the sad knowledge that with us things are not everywhere as they should be. With kindest regards, yours most sincerely,

ARNOLD SCHÖNBERG.'

Arnold Schoenberg, in a letter published in the *Daily Telegraph* (Jan 1914)

School Choirs

Philip Oakes describes a choir rehearsal at the Royal Orphanage School just before the outbreak of the Second World War:

'Apart from the air-raid drills there was no change in the school curriculum.... Preparations went ahead for Sports Day.... I was chosen for the choir which was to lead the entire school in a programme of songs conducted by Mr Gibbs. They included "The Mermaid" (in which Mr Gibbs was the soloist), a Gilbert and Sullivan selection and *"Non Nobis Domine"*. We rehearsed every day, except Saturdays and Sundays, for a month. Our rehearsals were the only times we could be sure we would not be interrupted by air-raid drills.... Mr Gibbs conducted in his shirt sleeves. Perfectly round beads of sweat appeared on his forehead as if it had been squeezed like orange peel ... music was the only subject which he seemed to take actual pleasure in teaching. He urged us to enjoy the exercise. "To sing is to make a joyful noise", he declared. "Let me hear joy in your voices." To encourage us he laughed up and down the scale, guffawing into our faces as if to make us inhale his enthusiasm. Close up he looked drunk. A gold tooth gleamed in his open mouth. His thinning hair which had come ungummed in the heat of the rehearsal shook as if it was stirred by a fan. His eyes bulged. He placed our hands on his belly so that we could feel the notes vibrate. It was like standing on the edge of a railway platform which began to tremble as the train approached.'

Philip Oakes *From Middle England – A Memory of the 1930's and 1940's* (1980)

Schubert, Franz (1797–1828)

'In the year 1822, Franz Schubert set out to present in person the master he honoured so highly, with his variations on a French song (opus 10). These variations he had previously dedicated to Beethoven. In spite of Diabelli accompanying him, and acting as spokesman and interpreter of Schubert's feelings, Schubert played a part in the interview which was anything but pleasant to him. His courage, which he managed to husband up to the very threshold of the house, forsook him entirely at the first glimpse he caught of the majestic artist; and when Beethoven expressed a wish that Schubert should write the answers to his questions, he felt as if his hands were tied and fettered. Beethoven ran through the presentation copy, and stumbled on some inaccuracy in harmony. He then, in the kindest manner, drew the young man's attention to the fault, adding that the fault was no deadly sin. Meantime the result of this remark, intended to be kind, was to utterly disconcert the nervous visitor. It was not until he got outside the house that Schubert recovered his equanimity, and rebuked him unsparingly.'

Although this interview distressed Schubert so considerably, the young composer had made a deep impression on Beethoven, and during his last days Beethoven studied Schubert's works with great interest. On his deathbed lay manuscript copies of some of Schubert's most famous songs. 'For several days he could not tear himself away from perusing them, and he pored for hours daily over the *Iphigénie, Grenzen der Menschheit, Die*

Allmacht, Die junge Nonne, Viola, the *Die schöne Müllerin* and several others. He exclaimed repeatedly, in a voice of rapturous delight, "Certainly a god-like spark dwells in Schubert! Had I had this poem, I, too, would have set it to music!" He could not say enough in praise of most of the other poems, and Schubert's original way of handling the subject.'

Anton F. Schindler *Beethoven as I Knew him* [1840], (1966)

At the close of the first movement of the Great C major Symphony, played in rehearsal under Dr Henry Wylde with the New Philharmonic Society's orchestra in 1852, the principal horn called out to one of the violinists:
    'Tom! Have you been able to discover a tune yet?'
    'I have *not*!' came the reply.

'Given time, he would probably have set the whole of German literature to music.'

Attributed to **Robert Schumann**

Schumann, Robert (1810–56)

'If you knew what these first joys of a composer were like. It would be right to compare them to the feelings of a bridegroom. All the sky of my heart is full of hope and joyful prophecies. The Doge of Venice, when he wedded the sea, was no prouder than I am when I celebrate for the first time my union with the vast world which is the world and the motherland of the artist.'

Robert Schumann, in a letter to his mother about the Abegg Variations (1829–30)

'If only you knew the ardour, the ferment that is in me and how I should have already arrived at Op. 100 with my symphonies, if only I had written them down! There are moments when music possesses me so completely, when only sounds exist for me to such a degree that I am unable to write anything down.'

Robert Schumann, in a letter to **Friedrich Wieck**

'Since yesterday morning I have written 27 pages of music of which all I can tell you is that, while composing them, I was laughing and crying with joy. . . . Farewell, my Clara! Sounds and music are killing me at this moment and I feel that I could die of them. Ah, Clara, what divine happiness there is in writing for the voice! . . . I would like to sing like the nightingale and die of it.'

Robert Schumann, in a letter to **Clara Wieck** while composing the song cycle **Liederkreis** (1840)

'The fanciful magic of this tone picture [Fantasy in C Major, op. 17], one of the most remarkable works of Schumann's *Sturm und Drang* period, had not been previously played in Vienna by anyone. In this Fantasy, Schumann originally had in mind a supplement to the Beethoven monument in Bonn, and he intended its three movements to represent the "Ruins", "Arch of Triumph", and "Wreath of Stars" of the monument. In subsequently abandoning this idea he robbed his disciples of an "interpretive" field-day. How unfailingly would the "thought-analysts" have heard Beethoven's whole biography in this piece, which now, without title, enjoys a certain immunity from such experiments!'

Eduard Hanslick *Music Criticisms 1846–99*, translated and edited by Henry Pleasants (1951)

'... Heine's poetry has many details in common with German Romantic poetry, but is lacking in the profound, limitless darkness of its ground-tone. We can best see ... what this dark tone is by listening to, or better, ourselves playing, Schumann's F Sharp Minor Sonata. We shall hear how the darkness of tone can combine with passionate day dreaming, often expressed with great cheerfulness. It is as if the cheerfulness necessarily follows from the abysmal darkness and fearlessly plunges into its depths, for "a heavy heart wears a cheerful countenance".... Yes, music expresses more clearly than words the many sided nature of German Romanticism....'

Max Brod *Heinrich Heine – The Artist in Revolt* (1956)

Schumann-Heink, Ernestine (1861–1936)

'The hearty meals consumed by some singers were often not due to greed but to the fact that they needed these calories to build up reserves of energy. Ernestine Schumann-Heink certainly required them for the Wagnerian roles in which she excelled. A friend once saw her in a restaurant with a huge steak before her. "Surely you aren't going to eat all that alone?" he asked. "No, not alone," she replied, "with potatoes, then apple pie and cream".'

Charles Neilson Gattey *The Elephant that Swallowed a Nightingale and Other Operatic Wonders* (1981)

Scottish Music

Sometimes, to hear people talk, you'd think all
    we had

Was bagpipe music and Hamish MacCunn's
    'Land of the Mountain and the Flood'.
No Scottish tradition of classical music? What
    tosh! In the top league
I can think of no less than three Scottish
    composers. Grieg   .25
Had a Scottish grandfather and Eugen d'Albert –
    don't be put off by the name
– whose verismo German opera 'Tiefland' has
    won such acclaim
Was 100% Scottish born and football-wise would
    have qualified   1.00
To play for Scotland had he not been a dwarf
    with six (consecutive) wives keeping
    him occupied.
Donizetti may well have been the son of a Scot
    named Don(ald) Izett   .5
And the ancestors of the founder of American
    composing Edward MacDowell didn't exactly
    hail from Tibet.   .25
How many know that the composer of such
    master works as 'Pièces en forme des
    petits pois'
The leader of L'Ecole d'Arceuil, Eric Satie, was the
    proud possessor of a Scottish ma?   .5
Or that to produce a virtuoso of the concerto
    grosso like Georg Muffat (1653–1704)
Generations upon generations of homegrown
    Dod Muffats had gone before?   .5
Who can tell how many Scots geniuses we might
    have had if they'd been a bit more teetotal.
But of top rank composers I think you'll agree this
    makes a fine wee total.   = 3

Robert Crozier 'A Notelet on Scottish Composers' (1983)

Shostakovich, Dimitry (1906–75)

'Shostakovich's own account of his "conversion" to a
better frame of mind more in accordance with the taste,
or lack of it, of Sovietical betters – is breathtaking in its
abjectness, its slavish prostration to authority, and is
such as no musician in the "bourgeois" capitalist West
was perhaps ever known to be guilty of before a
moneyed or aristocratic patron.'

Kaikhosru Shapurji Sorabji *Mi contra fa: the Immoralisings
of a Machiavellian Musician* (1947)

'Sorabji, in his diatribe against the Russian composer,
says that Shostakovich concludes that music can be
made, indeed *must* be made, to express an ideological
programme, and that it can have no existence apart from
such a programme. According to Sorabji, Shostakovich,
writing of the old masters, says: ''Whether they knew it

or not, they were bolstering the rule of the upper classes". Personally, I agree with Shostakovich there. Of the old masters, Beethoven seems the only one who directed his music to humanity and not some spiritual or temporal master.

Then Sorabji begins an explosive polemic in which he speaks of Shostakovich in terms of "nonconformist Pecksniffery gone mad" ... "this pretentious dunderhead, this ideology-besotted prig" ... "this preposterous personage" ... "this platitude-monger, this universal provider of the commonplace". To me this reads like the *Daily Express* at its worst. Sorabji doesn't often practise palinody, but I wish he would in this instance.'

Ronald Stevenson, in a conversation with Hugh MacDiarmid and John Ogdon, recorded in **Hugh MacDiarmid** *The Company I've Kept* (1966)

Sibelius, Jean (1865–1957)

'Sibelius's symphonies are very wayward at times, not too easy to grasp. Their style is so individual and so characteristic of the composer's remote Northern land that the somewhat severe outlines and quickly changing moods of the music cannot always be taken in at a first hearing. They are never *à la mode* and thus command the admiration and respect of those who are best able to assess their qualities. Of all the great writers since the last of the classical composers Sibelius is the one recognised by cultured musicians as the most fitting successor to the immortal Brahms ... he makes no concessions whatsoever to the cheap and tawdry tastes of the moment, his music being singularly free from sentimental harmony and from artificially clever and complex orchestration.'

Julius Harrison, in *The Musical Companion*, edited by A.L. Bacharach (1934)

'Here, for once, was a conductor who dared to take the symphony as slowly as the composer intended.... He played the slow movement like a bard of old ... the movement towered ... it had in it something of the large utterance of the early gods.'

Olin Downes, writing of a performance of Sibelius's Second Symphony conducted by Sir Malcolm Sargent, in the *New York Times*; quoted in **Charles Reid** *Malcolm Sargent: a Biography* (1968)

Singers

The tenor's voice is spoilt by affectation,
And for the bass, the beast can only bellow;

In fact, he had no singing education,
An ignorant, noteless, timeless, tuneless fellow.

George Byron *Don Juan*, Canto IV, stanza 87 (1819–24)

Swans sing before they die – 'twere no bad thing
Should certain persons die before they sing.

Samuel Taylor Coleridge (1772–1834) *Epigram on a Volunteer Singer*

'Tenors are noble, pure and heroic and get the soprano, if she has not tragically expired before the final curtain. But baritones are born villains in opera.'

Leonard Warren, quoted in the *New York World-Telegram* (13 March 1957)

'Oh how wonderful, really wonderful, opera would be – if there were no singers!'

Attributed to **Gioachino Rossini**

'*Tosca in Tokyo* featured Montserrat Caballé. The Japanese were impressed. It was clear that they hadn't seen anything that size since the battleship *Missouri* anchored in Tokyo Bay in 1945.'

Clive James, in *The Observer* (14 Oct 1979)

'What makes the difference between an opera of Mozart's and the singing of a thrush confined in a wooden cage at the corner of the street? The one is nature, and the other is art; the one is paid for, and the other is not. Madame Foder sang the air of *Vedrai Carino* in *Don Giovanni* so divinely, because she was hired to sing it; she sang it to please the audience, not herself, and did not always like to be *encored* ... but the thrush that awakes us at daybreak with its song, does not sing because it is paid to sing, or to please others, or to be admired or criticised. It sings because it is happy: it pours the thrilling sounds from its throat, to relieve the overflowing of its own heart. ... That stream of joy comes pure and fresh to the longing sense, free from art and affectation.'

William Hazlitt 'Notes of a Journey Through France and Italy', in the *Morning Chronicle* (1825)

'God in His Almighty Wisdom and Fairness has not always given the greatest voices to the persons with the greatest intellect or the best education, or to the most beautiful of his creatures.'

Tyrone Guthrie *A Life in the Theatre* (1960)

'She was a singer who had to take any note above A with her eyebrows.'

Montague Glass (1877–1934)

'All singers have this fault: if asked to sing among friends they are never so inclined; if unasked, they never leave off.'

Horace *Satires*

''Tis the common disease of all your musicians, that they never know no mean, to be entreated either to begin or end.'

Ben Jonson *The Poetaster*, Act II, scene i (1601)

'The orchestra should support the singer as the sea does a boat.'

Richard Wagner, quoted in **Heinrich Porges** *Wagner Rehearsing 'The Ring'* (1983)

Singing

First, [singing] is a knowledge easily taught, and quickly learned, where there is a good master, and an apt scholar.

2. The exercise of singing is delightful to Nature, and good to preserve the health of Man.

3. It doth strengthen all parts of the breast, and doth open the pipes.

4. It is a singular good remedy for stuttering and stammering in the speech.

4. It is the best means to procure a perfect pronunciation, and to make a good orator.

6. It is the only way to know where Nature hath bestowed the benefit of a good voice: which gift is so rare, as there is not one among a thousand, that hath it: and in many, that excellent gift is lost, because they want Art to express Nature.

7. There is not any music of instruments whatsoever, comparable to that which is made of the voices of Men, where the voices are good, and the same well sorted and ordered.

8. The better the voice is, the meeter it is to honour and God therewith: and the voice of man is chiefly to be employed to that end.

Since singing is so good a thing,
I wish all men would learn to sing.

William Byrd *Psalmes, Sonets and Songs of Sadness and Pietie* (1588)

'Intense was the low murmur of admiration when a particularly small gentleman, in a dress coat, led on a particularly tall lady in a blue sarcenet pelisse and bonnet of the same, ornamented with large white feathers, and forthwith commenced a plaintive duet.... It was a beautiful duet: first the small gentleman asked a question, and then the tall lady answered it; then the small gentleman and the tall lady sang together most melodiously; then the small gentleman went through a little piece of vehemence by himself, and got very tenor indeed, in the excitement of his feelings, to which the tall lady responded in a similar manner; then the small gentleman had a shake [trill] or two, after which the tall lady had the same, and then they both merged imperceptibly into the original air: and the band wound themselves up to a pitch of fury, and the small gentleman handed the tall lady out, and the applause was rapturous.'

Charles Dickens, describing an operatic duet sung during a public concert at the Vauxhall Gardens in 1834, in *Sketches by Boz* (1835)

'I have never met a single German Kapellmeister or musical-director who could really *sing* a melody, be his voice good or bad. No, music to them is an abstraction, a mixture of syntax, arithmetic and gymnastics. . . .

The human voice is the practical foundation of music, and however far the latter may progress upon the path of its choice, the boldest expressions of the composer or the most daring bravura of the instrumental virtuoso must always return to the essence of song for its ultimate vindication. Thus I maintain that elementary instruction in singing must be made obligatory for every musician, and in the successful organisation of a singing-school upon these lines should be found the basis for the intended all-embracing school of music. Only then should it extend frontiers which it has been seen to reach with the need to instruct the singer in the elements of harmony and rudimentary analysis of musical composition.'

Richard Wagner 'On Conducting', in *Richard Wagner's Prose Works*, edited and translated by **William Ashton Ellis** 4 (1895)

The entire overture, long as it was, was played to a dark house with the curtain down. It was exquisite; it was delicious. But straightway thereafter, of course, came the singing, and it does seem to me that nothing can make a Wagner opera absolutely perfect and satisfactory to the untutored but to leave out the vocal parts. I wish I could see a Wagner opera done in pantomime once. Then one would have the lovely orchestration unvexed to listen to and bathe his spirit in, and the bewildering beautiful scenery to intoxicate his eyes with, and the dumb acting couldn't mar these pleasures, because there isn't often anything in the Wagner opera that one would call by such a violent name as acting; as a rule all you would see would be a couple of silent people, one of them standing still, the other catching flies. Of course I do not really mean that he would be catching flies; I only mean that the usual operatic gestures which consist in reaching first one hand out into the air and then the other might suggest the sport I speak of if the operator attended strictly to business and uttered no sound.

This present opera was 'Parsifal'. Madame Wagner does not permit its representation anywhere but in Bayreuth. The first act of the three occupied two hours, and I enjoyed that in spite of the singing.

I trust that I know as well as anybody that singing is one of the most entrancing and bewitching and moving and eloquent of all the vehicles invented by man for the conveying of feeling; but it seems to me that the chief virtue in song is melody, air, tune, rhythm, or what you please to call it, and that when this feature is absent what remains is a picture with the color left out. I was not able to detect in the vocal parts of 'Parsifal' anything that might with confidence be called rhythm or tune or melody; one person performed at a time – and a long time, too – often in a noble, and always in a high-toned, voice; but he only pulled out long notes, then some short ones, then another long one, then a sharp, quick, peremptory bark or two – and so on and so on; and when he was done you saw that the information which he had conveyed had not compensated for the disturbance. Not always, but pretty often. If two of them would but put in a duet occasionally and blend the voices; but no, they don't do that. The great master, who knew so well how to make a hundred instruments rejoice in unison and pour out their souls in mingled and melodious tides of delicious sounds, deals only in barren solos when he puts in the vocal parts. It may be that he was deep, and only added the singing to his operas for the sake of the contrast it would make with the music. Singing! It does seem the wrong name to apply to it. Strictly described, it is a practising of difficult and unpleasant intervals, mainly. An ignorant person gets tired of listening to gymnastic intervals in the long run, no matter how pleasant they may be.

Mark Twain, recounting a visit to the Bayreuth Festival in 1891, in 'At the Shrine of St Wagner', *New York Sun* (1891)

Snobbery

He thinks the great composers were like him.
Regards them as soul-brothers, tuneful bores.
He has their measure, pores over their scores,
Collects concertos, shakes his head through sym-

phonies and nightly puts on a cassette
Of Stockhausen to lull him into sleep.
His office chums regard him as a creep;
The girls condemn him as a sopping wet.

Still, come the concert he is in the mood:
He simpers over Monteverdi chants

As others drool for Adam and the Ants.
He turns his nose up at the common crowd.

For shallow sods like him, would you believe,
Poor Mozart ended in a pauper's grave.

F. Scott Monument *The Muzak Snob* (1982)

Sousa, John Philip (1854–1932)

'He wrote marches for this [US Marine] band, including *Stars and Stripes Forever*, a neatly assembled flame of controlled fire, guaranteed to make the lame walk.'

Ian Whitcomb *After the Ball: Popular Song from Rag to Rock* (1972)

'Sousa was no Beethoven. Nonetheless, he was Sousa.'

Deems Taylor *Of Men and Music* (1937)

'In certain of his strains he struck an incomparably popular and vital note. He said the national thing in a certain way that no one else ever achieved, and that could be said only of this nation.... There is national braggadocio of the imperialistic era; Uncle Sam in his striped hat, goatee, and trousers, out to lick the world, by gum.'

Olin Downes, quoted in *Olin Downes on Music*, edited by **Irene Downes** (1957)

Sparta

There was a young fellow from Sparta,
A really magnificent farter,
    On the strength of one bean
    He'd fart God Save the Queen,
And Beethoven's Moonlight Sonata.

He was great in the Christmas Cantata,
He could double-stop fart the Toccata,
    He'd boom from his ass
    Bach's B Minor Mass,
And, in counterpoint, La Traviata.

Traditional, quoted in **G. Legman** (ed) *The Limerick: 1700 Examples, With Notes, Variants and Index* (1969)

Stanford, Charles Villiers (1852–1924)

'Stanford's Irish birth and English upbringing blend attractively in his work. He is a natural singer with a much readier gift for a memorable tune than we ever find in Parry.... The influence of Brahms, whom he revered, is sometimes too plainly evident in the chamber music to make it quite convincing as an individual enlargement of the repertory.... What he lacks is fantasy, sometimes even poetry.... He narrowly missed, one cannot quite tell why, becoming an Irish Dvořák, as Mackenzie missed, rather less narrowly, being a Scottish national representative of that stature.'

Eric Blom *Music in England* (1942)

Stockhausen, Karlheinz (born 1928)

In one apochryphal tale, Sir Thomas Beecham was once asked if he had ever played any Stockhausen. 'No,' he is said to have replied, 'but I have trodden in some.'

Stokowski, Leopold (1882–1977)

'He was one of the few conductors Otto Klemperer admired.'

Lord Harewood, in *The Tongs and the Bones: the Memoirs of Lord Harewood* (1981)

Strauss, Johann, The Younger (1825–99)

Strauss's daughter asked Johannes Brahms for his autograph. In her autograph book the composer wrote the opening bars of the *Blue Danube* waltz, and beneath them the words 'Not, alas, by Johannes Brahms'.

Strauss, Richard (1864–1949)

'He who desires no more from an orchestral piece than that it transport him to the dissolute ecstasy of a Don Juan, panting for everything feminine, may well find pleasure in this music, for with its exquisite skilfulness it achieves the desired objective in so far as it is musically attainable. The composer may thus be compared with a routined chemist who well understands how to mix all the elements of musical-sensual stimulation to produce a stupefying "pleasure gas". For my part, I prefer, with all due homage to such chemical skill, not to be its victim.'

Eduard Hanslick, reviewing the first performance of the tone poem *Don Juan*, under Hans Richter, at a Philharmonic concert in Vienna on 10 January 1892

'Those who are called upon to discuss the version of *Salome* presented at Covent Garden last night, with the consent of the Lord Chamberlain, are placed in this dilemma – either they must judge the music in its relation to the revised text – in which case the dramatic, psychological, and social aspects of Strauss and Wilde's conceptions are almost wholly lost – or the characters on the stage must be regarded as saying one thing and meaning another. . . . With the exception of the Prophet's music, the interest is none too well maintained up to the moment of the now famous Dance of the Seven Veils, which is not as rhythmically sensual as has been said. There is a lot of ugly music, as perhaps befits an ugly subject, and, needless to say, numerous realistic effects. . . . The apostrophe to the head is very tuneful, if not a little ordinary, though . . . in this instance there is no head to apostrophise. . . . It does justice to neither Wilde nor Strauss, to Mr. Beecham, nor his artists, and it will fail to satisfy purist, prude or prurient.'

Review of the first London performance of *Salome* (in a modified version) conducted by Thomas Beecham, in *The Standard* (9 Dec 1910)

'[*Der Rosenkavalier*] is of all waltzes all compact, and those waltzes are so luscious, so danceable and so insinuating that they recall once more the glorious days of *The Gypsy Baron, Die Fledermaus*. . . . Strauss, in brief, has stepped into the vacant post of waltz-king. . . . Hereafter, we'll shake our legs, at rout and maskerade, to the music of the future.'

H.L. Mencken 'Der Rosenkavalier', in the *Evening Sun* (31 Jan 1911)

Claude Debussy gives his impressions of the symphony concert conducted by Richard Strauss which included the second performance in Paris of *Ein Heldenleben*:
   '. . . One may not care for certain experiments which border on the commonplace or for a kind of tortured Italianism; but after a minute or two one is captured first by the tremendous versatility of his orchestration, then by the frenzied energy which carries one with him for as long as he chooses; the hearer is no longer master of his emotions, he does not even notice that his symphonic poem exceeds the limits that our patience usually allows to such compositions . . . it is a book of pictures, or even a cinematograph. But one must admit that the man who composed such a work at so continuously high a pressure is very nearly a genius.
   He began by giving *Italy*, a symphonic fantasy in four parts – an early work, I believe – where the future originality of Strauss is already discernible. . . . Then came a love scene from *Feuersnot*. . . . This suffered considerably through being detached from its context. . . .

Richard Strauss has no wild lock of hair, no epileptic gestures. He is tall and he has the free and determined bearing of those great explorers who journey among savage tribes with a smile on their lips. Perhaps this sort of bearing is necessary to shake the conventionality of the public. He has, however, the head of a musician; but his eyes and gestures are those of a Superman, to quote Nietzsche. . . . From Nietzsche too he must have learned his lofty scorn of feeble sentimentalities and his desire that music should not go on for ever providing a more or less satisfactory illumination for our nights, but that it should shine like the sun. I can assure you that there is sunshine in the music of Strauss. Unquestionably the majority of the audience did not like sunshine of this kind, for quite famous musical enthusiasts showed unmistakable signs of impatience. But that did not prevent Strauss from being greeted with rapturous applause. . . .'

Claude Debussy *Monsieur Croche the Dilettante Hater* (1928)

Sir Thomas Beecham used to maintain that as a master of the orchestra Richard Strauss could not hold a candle to Puccini, who had 'everybody licked'.

'I once spent a couple of days in the train with a German friend of mine. We amused ourselves by discovering how many notes we could take out of *Heldenleben* and leave the music essentially intact. By the time we finished we had taken out 15,000.'

Sir Thomas Beecham, quoted in **Charles Reid** *Beecham: an Independent Biography* (1961)

Stravinsky, Igor (1882–1972)

'One is reminded instantly of Picasso. So much of the music is aurally the equivalent of Picasso's perversions of natural form. Listening to certain of Stravinsky's "misplaced" pedal points is like looking at a nose growing in profile from the ear of a Picasso full-face portrait. I am not at present . . . concerned to defend Picasso's peculiar line in plastic surgery. Certainly, however, I find its musical counterpart in *Pulcinella* exquisite.'

Charles Stuart 'Russia and Music', in *Music 1950*, edited by Ralph Hill (1950)

The first performance of *The Rite of Spring* by the Russian Ballet at the Théâtre des Champs-Elysées, Paris, on 29 May 1913 was one of the scandals of twentieth-century music-making:

'a certain part of the audience was thrilled by what it considered to be a blasphemous attempt to destroy music as an art, and, swept away with wrath, began, very soon after the rise of the curtain, to make cat-calls

and to offer audible suggestions as to how the performance should proceed. The orchestra played unheard,
except occasionally when a slight lull occurred. The
young man seated behind me in the box stood up ... to
enable himself to see more clearly. The intense excitement under which he was labouring betrayed itself
presently when he began to beat rhythmically on top of
my head with his fists. My emotion was so great that I
did not feel the blows for some time.'

Carl van Vechten, quoted in **Eric Walter White** *Stravinsky
– The Composer and his Works* (1979)

'In every note of his music Stravinsky celebrates the
unknowability, the darkness, that lies at the heart of
nature, asserting through his intuitive and even partly
unconscious perception ... a fact that is becoming more
and more apparent in our own time.... To know that
there are things that one cannot, and even need not,
know is to be able to live once more in a world of rich and
varied meaning.'

Christopher Small *Music – Society – Education* (1977)

'I liked the opera very much. Everything but the music.'

Benjamin Britten, speaking to W.H. Auden of
Stravinsky's *The Rake's Progress*

Street Music

'Nothing is talked of but feasts and dances; and in all
public places, violins, hautbois, and other sorts of
instruments are so common, for the amusement of
particular persons, that at all hours of the day, one may
have one's ears charmed with their sweet melody.'

Sieur de la Serre *Pleasures of London* (1639)

'We heard a noise so dreadful and surprising, that we
thought the Devil was riding or hunting through the
City, with a pack of deep-mouth'd hell-hounds.... At
last bolted out from the corner of a street ... a parcel of
strange hobgoblins cover'd with long frize rugs and
blankets, hoop'd round with leather girdles from their
cruppers to their shoulders and their noodles button'd
up into caps of martial figure ... one arm'd, as I thought,
with a lusty faggot-bat, and the rest with strange wooden
weapons in their hands in the shape of clyster-pipes, but
as long, almost, as speaking trumpets. Of a sudden they
clapp'd them to their mouths, and made such a frightful
yelling that I thought the world had been dissolving, and
the terrible sound of the last trumpet to be within an inch
of my ears.... I ask'd my friend what was the meaning
of this infernal outcry? Prithee, says he, what's the

matter with thee? ... Why, these are the City Waites, who play every winter's night through the streets, to rouse each lazy drone to family duty.... These are the Topping Tooters of the Town.'

Ned Ward *The London Spy* (1698–1709)

'... numbers of street musicians [playing by ear] are better instrumentalists than many educated musicians.... All the street-performers of wind instruments are short-lived. Wind performers drink more, too, than the others. They must have their mouths wet, and they need more stimulant or restorative after blowing an hour in the streets. There are now twice as many wind as stringed instruments played in the streets; 15 or 16 years ago there used to be more stringed instruments. Within that time new wind instruments have been used in the streets. Cornopeans, or cornet-a-pistons, came into vogue about 14 years ago; ophicleides about 10 years ago (I'm speaking about the streets); and saxhorns about two years since. The cornopean has now quite superceded the bugle. The worst part of the street performers, in point of character, are those who play before or in public-houses. They drink a great deal, but I never heard of them being charged with dishonesty. In fact, I believe there's no honester set of men breathing than street musicians.'

A street musician of 26, interviewed by Henry Mayhew, in *London Labour and the London Poor* (1861)

'There is a nuisance common enough with us about the streets; and in London it takes every shape. I mean street music. Besides the troops, which infest public places, startling you with a crashing outburst of noise from many brass instruments, there are mendicants, of all ages and both sexes. The halt, the blind, come singing in the most doleful manner, unaccompanied; and others making the night hideous with squeaking wind-pipes, or noisy things of some sort.'

Ah-Chin-Le *Some Observations upon the Civilization of the Western Barbarians* (1876)

'Almost always in London – in the congregated uproar of streets, or in the noise that drifts through walls and windows – you can hear the hackneyed melancholy of street-music; a music which sounds like the actual voice of the human heart, singing the lost joys, the regrets, the loveless lives of the people who blacken the pavements, or jolt along on the buses.

"Speak to me kindly," the hand-organ implores; "I am all alone!" it screams amid the throngs. "Thy vows are all broken," it laments in dingy courtyards, "And Light is Thy Fame." And of hot summer afternoons, the Cry for Courage to Remember, or Calmness to Forget, floats in with the smell of paint and asphalt through open office windows.'

Logan Pearsall Smith *Trivia* (1918)

A barrel-organ's playing somewhere in a London street,
As the sun sinks low,
Though the music's only Verdi, yet the melody is sweet.

Alfred Noyes (1880–1958) *Barrel-organ*

Sullivan, Sir Arthur (1842–1900)

'They trained him to make Europe yawn; and he took advantage of their teaching to make London and New York laugh and whistle.'

George Bernard Shaw, in the *Scots Observer* (6 Sep 1890)

'I was one of the few who thought that [Sullivan's] great popularity had really harmed his genius. . . . Gilbert's wit didn't go very deep, whereas the music of Sullivan was of the very first order. One forgets today the splendid *Golden Legend* to remember that the music of *Onward, Christian Soldiers* is his; but he also wrote *The Martyr of Antioch* and *The Light of the World*, and is certainly the first of all English musicians – greater even than Purcell.'

Frank Harris *My Life and Loves* (1925)

'I don't pretend to know much about music, but I do know I have been listening to a very great work.'

Charles Dickens, on hearing Sullivan's *The Tempest* in 1862; quoted in **Hesketh Pearson** *Gilbert and Sullivan* (1935)

'If Sterndale Bennett, in his time, was a tired, listless conductor, his successor, Sir Arthur Sullivan, is a veritable nightcap ... there is a phlegmatism, probably unique. Sullivan presides on the podium from the comfortable recesses of a commodious arm-chair, his left arm lazily extended on the arm-rest, his right giving the beat in a mechanical way, his eyes fastened to the score. . . . Sullivan never looked up from the notes; it was as though he was reading at sight. . . . At the end the audience applauded long and loudly, but it apparently never occurred to Sullivan to turn round and face the audience.'

Eduard Hanslick *Music Criticisms 1846–99* (1963)

'Sullivan has been gaining ground and Gilbert losing it since they died. The reason is that when they started Gilbert was new and unique; he had absolutely no rivals. But Sullivan was hard up against Offenbach, whose music was like champagne, and also against Auber, whose *Fra Diavolo* was a masterpiece. Sullivan was a church organist; and when I in my teens heard *Trial by Jury* ... its harmonies struck me as most unexpectedly churchy after Offenbach. Offenbach and Auber are now forgotten; and Sullivan's music is as light as air beside Elgar's or Prokofieff's.'

George Bernard Shaw, in a letter to Hesketh Pearson; quoted in *Gilbert and Sullivan* (1935)

Sutherland, Dame Joan (born 1926)

'Joan Sutherland, as Donna Anna [in Mozart's *Don Giovanni*], made a fleeting moment of Glyndebourne history when, at the dress rehearsal, with the connivance of the conductor and according to the intentions of the composer, she let fly a short cadenza during the silent pause in her aria, "Or sai chi l'onore". It goes without saying that this joyous moment was short-lived, for Glyndebourne, so lavish in so many ways, would not tolerate this departure from its austere, immovable observance of the letter of Mozart's scores. The cadenza was never allowed again. But there is no doubt that Miss Sutherland was absolutely right to introduce it and that Mr. Pritchard was right to encourage it. It is no good anybody pretending that the silent pauses in Mozart's arias are pauses for "dramatic effect".... These pauses were put in for the singer to fill up, and when Mozart didn't want them filled ... he suggested moderation by writing into the part what he considered was enough.... It has always seemed a little illogical to me to permit the cadenzas in *Macbeth*, and even later operas of Verdi, merely because the composer wrote them down, but to forbid them in Mozart, who didn't write them down, because they were a flourishing convention which the composer expected his performers to observe and enjoy.'

Spike Hughes *Glyndebourne: a History of the Festival Opera* (1965)

Szell, George (1897–1970)

'He has an enormously wide repertory. He can conduct anything, provided it's by Beethoven, Brahms or Wagner. He tried Debussy's *La mer* once. It came out as *Das Merde*.'

Attributed to an American orchestral player

Someone once commented in the hearing of Rudolf Bing, general manager of the Metropolitan Opera, New York: 'Georg Szell is his own worst enemy'. 'Not while I'm alive, he isn't!' Rudolf Bing said.

Taste

'What is the voice of song, when the world lacks the ear of taste?'

Nathaniel Hawthorne *The Snow Image: Canterbury Pilgrims* (1852)

'I distinctly saw six people in the stalls, probably with complimentary tickets. . . .

The occasion was infinitely more important than the Derby, than Goodwood, than the Cup Finals, than the Carpentier fights, than any of the occasions on which the official leaders of society are photographed and cinematographed laboriously shaking hands with persons on whom Molière's patron, Louis XIV, and Bach's patron, Frederick the Great, would not have condescended to wipe their boots. . . .

I apologise to posterity for living in a country where the capacity and tastes of schoolboys and sporting costermongers are the measure of metropolitan culture. . . .'

George Bernard Shaw, on the attendance at a performance of Elgar's *The Apostles* at the Queen's Hall in 1922; quoted in **Hesketh Pearson** *Bernard Shaw: his Life and Personality* (1942)

'In art as in religion we are apt to discover what we hope to find, to judge the source by the extent to which it supplies our own thirst.'

Sir Jack Westrup *Purcell* (1937)

'it is the devotees of the latest thing who are themselves enslaved to all the vices of which they accuse the rest of us. They are the real provincials and the real conformists. Because they are too ignorant to know anything about any age except the one in which they live, they accept all its atrocities at face value, and because they have no taste or judgement of their own, they admire the things – and only the things – that those who happen to have caught the ear of the age tell them it is safe to admire. Even I can remember when Verdi was definitely "out"; now he is as "in" as Bach and Wagner themselves.'

Edward Wagenknecht *As Far as Yesterday: Memories and Reflections* (1968)

Tchaikovsky, Pyotr Il'yich (1840–93)

'If you had asked me whether I had ever found complete happiness in love, I should have replied no, and again, no. Besides, I think the answer to this question is to be heard in my music. If, however, you ask me whether I have felt the whole power and inexpressible stress of love, I must reply, yes, yes, yes; for often I have striven to render in music all the anguish and the bliss of love.'

Pyotr Il'yich Tchaikovsky, in a letter to Nadezhda von Meck

'In this grand complex of tunes [the "Pathétique" Symphony], Tchaikowsky tells us all his troubles – how he was forced into marriage against his will; how he lost three thousand roubles on Russian Government bonds; how his pet dog Wolfgang was run over by the Moscow–Petersburg D-*Zug* and lost an ear; how the concertmaster was in liquor at Dresden and spoiled his *Romeo and Juliet*; how ill he was after eating that *gekochter Schellfisch* at Prague; how the wine merchant, Oroshatovich, swindled him with synthetic Burgundy; how he lost his baggage between Leipzig and Berlin, and had to conduct in borrowed cuffs; how the summer boarders at Maidanovo played "Monastery Bells" on their tin-pan pianos; how that *Schuft* of a critic at Köln accused him of borrowing his Capriccio in G sharp minor from Offenbach; how his friend Kashkin won a hundred roubles from him at *yeralash*; how he cut his hand opening a can of asparagus; how melancholy it was to come to fifty-year. . . .'

H.L. Mencken *'If You Have Tears to Shed – !'*, in *Evening Sun* (6 Dec 1916)

'. . . so many people, who are neither simple, nor naive, nor spontaneous, seek in their art simplicity, "poverty", and spontaneity. Chaikowsky in his very nature possessed these three gifts to the fullest extent. That is why he never feared to let himself go, whereas the prudes, whether *raffinés* or academic, were shocked by the frank speech, free from artifice, of his music.

Chaikowsky possessed the power of *melody*, centre of gravity in every symphony, opera or ballet composed by him. It is absolutely indifferent to me that the quality of his melody was sometimes unequal. The fact is that he was a creator of *melody*, which is an extremely rare and precious gift. . . . And that is something which is not German. The Germans manufactured and manufactured music with themes and *Leitmotive* which they substitute for melodies.

Chaikowsky's music, which does not appear specifically Russian to everybody, is often more profoundly Russian than music which has long since been awarded the facile label of Muscovite picturesqueness. . . . While not specifically cultivating in his art the "soul of the Russian peasant", Chiakowsky drew *unconsciously* from the true, popular sources of our race." '

Igor Stravinsky, Open Letter to Serge Diaghilev, *The Times*, 18 Oct 1921

Thomson, Virgil (born 1896)

'Musical society consists of musicians who compose and musicians who do not. Those who do not are called "musical artists", "interpreters", "executants" or merely "musicians". Those who do compose have all been executants at one time or another. One only learns to create performable works of music by first learning to perform. The longevity of musical works, however, is dependent upon their being performable by executants other than the composer. . . .

Music is different from both poetry and painting in this respect. A musical manuscript is not music in the way that a written poem is poetry. It is merely a project for execution. It can correctly be said to consist of "notes" and to require "interpretation". It has about the same relation to real music that an architect's plan has to a real building. It is not a finished product. Auditive execution is the only possible test of its value.'

Virgil Thomson *The State of Music*, 2nd edition (1962)

Tone-deafness

'All animated nature loves music, except myself!'

Samuel Johnson, quoted in **Sir John Hawkins** *Johnsonia* (1787–9)

'I took leave and went to hear Mrs. Turner's daughter . . . play on the harpsichord; but Lord, it was enough to make any man sick to hear her; yet I was forced to commend her highly.'

Samuel Pepys *Diary*, entry for 1 May 1663

'I know only two tunes. One of them is *Yankee Doodle*, and the other isn't.'

Attributed to **General Ulysses S. Grant**

'Isaac Newton, hearing Handel play upon the harpsichord, could find nothing worthy to remark but the elasticity of his fingers.'

Quoted in *The Works of Alexander Pope*, edited by **Joseph Warton** (1797)

'She doesn't like instrumental music and only attends long concerts like these to please her husband.'

Richard Wagner, in a letter to his wife Cosima, after meeting Queen Victoria during his season with the Philharmonic Society in London in 1855

'Pope was so very insensible to the charms of music that he once asked Dr. Arbuthnot whether the rapture which the company expressed upon hearing the compositions and performance of Handel did not proceed wholly from affectation.'

Quoted in *The Works of Alexander Pope*, edited by **Joseph Warton** (1797)

'. . . we went to Jenny Lind's concert, for which a gentleman here gave us tickets, and at the end of the first act we agreed to come away. It struck me as atrociously stupid. I was thinking of something else the whole time she was jugulating away, and O!! I was so glad to get to the end and have a cigar.'

William Makepiece Thackeray, in a letter to Mrs Brookfield of 1850

Bottom: I have a reasonable good ear in music. Let's have the tongs and the bones.

William Shakespeare *A Midsummer Night's Dream*, Act IV, scene i (1595)

'I am constitutionally susceptible of noises. A carpenter's hammer, in a warm summer noon, will fret me into more than midsummer madness. But those unconnected, unset sounds are nothing to the measured malice of music. . . .'

'I even think that sentimentally I am disposed to harmony. But organically I am incapable of a tune.'

Charles Lamb *Essays of Elia – A Chapter on Ears*

Charles Darwin, author of *The Origin of Species by Means of Natural Selection*, deeply loved music and, what is more, responded to it with actual physical ecstasy. Hearing the anthems in King's College Chapel actually made his backbone shiver, he claimed. He got deep delight from the full harmonies of the symphonic music of Mozart and Beethoven, and yet he was obviously tone-deaf. This puzzled him.

'I am so utterly destitute of an ear, that I cannot perceive a discord, or keep time and hum a tune correctly; and it is a mystery how I could possibly have derived pleasure from music.'

Charles Darwin, quoted in **Peter Brent** *Charles Darwin: a Man of Enlarged Curiosity* (1981)

'I am quite indifferent to serious music, and I should not suffer from any sense of loss if all the scores of all the operas that have ever been written, and all the persons who might be able to reconstruct them from memory, were to perish in a sudden holocaust to-morrow. And yet I like going to Covent Garden. In June and July it is not the least pleasant mode of whiling away the half hour between dinner and supper. With its cool vestibules and colonnades and *foyers*, Covent Garden, despite its humble site and comparatively mean proportions, is an ideal place for a cigarette. Merely to wander behind the Grand Tier and read the illustrious names printed on the doors and boxes ... is an experience to thrill hearts that are far less snobbishly impressionable than my heart is. I seem to breathe, with every step I take in that circuit, the tart ozone of distinction. The sultriness of no night in summer can rob me of the exhilaration which fills my being in that most high and rarefied and buoyant atmosphere. I seem to tread the circuit with very light feet. Soon I am of a mood for the auditorium. As I pass down one of the narrow stairways leading to that sea of sleek heads and jewelled or feathered *coiffures*, the stalls, a stout gentleman unconsciously obstructs my path. As he makes way for me, I recognise in him, from an old drawing in *Punch*, an hereditary legislator who was once in one of Mr. Gladstone's Cabinets. *En passant*, I tread upon his foot, that I may have the honour of apologising to him. He bows courteously. I am happy. On the vast and cavernous stage, behind low-burning footlights, some opera or other is proceeding. The fiddlers are fiddling in a quiet monotone, not loud enough to drown the chatter in the stalls and boxes. All around me the people are chattering to one another like so many smart apes. Snatches of discussion here, and of flirtation there, are wafted past me, gaily, ceaselessly. I see the flash of eager gestures in white kid; I see white shoulders, white gardenias, rouge under lurid oeiliads, the quivering of *aigrettes*, the light on high collars highly polished and the sheen of innumerable diamonds, and the rhythmic sway of a thousand-and-one fans. Row upon row, the little dull-red boxes, receptacles of a bravery and beauty, are sparkling, also, with ceaseless animation. To me they are like an exquisite panorama of Punch-and-Judy shows. Every lady, I think, should bring her lap dog and set it on the ledge of her box, to consummate the illusion.'

Max Beerbohm *More* (1899)

Toscanini, Arturo (1867–1957)

Zinka Milanov, the Yugoslavian soprano, was one of the greatest Verdi sopranos of this century. She had already earned a huge reputation at the opera in Zagreb from 1928, but her astounding performance in Verdi's Requiem under Toscanini at the Salzburg Festival in 1937 led to her appearance at the Metropolitan Opera, and an international career. She had an ample bosom. Driven to the point of desperation during a rehearsal, Toscanini said to her: 'Oh, madam, if only those were brains, you would be the greatest soprano of all.'

Quoted in **Charles Neilson Gatty** *The Elephant that Swallowed a Nightingale and other Operatic Wonders* (1981)

'Almost every conductor is known to the orchestra by some little mannerism or catchword.... Toscanini's unceasing cry, "Singing, cantando, ah, cantando sempre! Always cantare!" echoes long after the others. This one word "cantando" expresses all that he desires so intensely from his orchestra.'

Bernard Shore *The Orchestra Speaks* (1938)

'A reactionary in spirit, [Toscanini] has nonetheless revolutionized orchestral conducting by his radical simplification of its procedures. Almost wholly devoted to the playing of familiar classics, he has at the same time transformed these into an auditive image of twentieth century America with such unconscious completeness that musicians and laymen all over the world have acclaimed his achievement without, I think, very much bothering to analyze it.'

Virgil Thomson *The Musical Scene* (1945)

'The man was supercharged; and it permeated the atmosphere, creating an aura of excitement that we didn't feel with other conductors. A concert can be a concert, or it can be a concert plus an event; and with Toscanini we had the double feature. But it was the dress rehearsals that were absolutely extraordinary: in that atmosphere of quiet and intense concentration we were hypnotized, and the ninety-five men functioned as one.'

Bernard H. Haggin *The Toscanini Musicians Knew* (1967)

'To stop a telephone bell ringing during a private rehearsal with Menuhin, Toscanini pulled the instrument from the wall, plaster and all, and returned without a word to the piano. No one expressed any surprise, though Menuhin confessed that he had never before seen such an uninhibited obedience to impulse.'

The Times (17 Jan 1957)

'His creative attitude to his work in the theatre is illustrated by his remarks to a violinist during a rehearsal of the overture to *Traviata*. One phrase was not to his liking, and eventually he burst out: "But can't you read what it says? It's quite plainly written down".
    "It says *Lamentoso*," answered the player.
    "Well, weep then, *weep*, in the name of God!"'

Filippo Sacchi *The Magic Baton* (1957)

'I hate Toscanini. I've never heard him in a concert hall, but I've heard enough of his recordings. What he does to music is terrible.... He chops it up into a hash and then pours a disgusting sauce over it.... I've read about Toscanini's conducting style and his manner of conducting a rehearsal.... I think it's outrageous.... He screams and curses the musicians and makes scenes in the most shameless manner. The poor musicians have to put up with all this nonsense.... And they even begin to see "something in it".'

Dmitry Shostakovich *Testimony: the Memoirs of Dmitri Shostakovich* (1979)

Trombone

'the sackbut or trombone ... being furnished with a slide ... had greater facility of execution and could therefore modulate from the key during the progress of the music, an advantage not shared by either trumpet or horn. But as the popularity of the French horn increased, so the trombone seems to have gone temporarily out of fashion. In Henry VIII's band we find ten trombones; in Elizabeth's, four; and, by Handel's time, there was scarcely a player to be found in all England.'

Julius Harrison 'The Orchestra and Orchestral Music', in *The Musical Companion*, edited by **A.L. Bacharach** (1934)

'At the new Theatre in the Haymarket this day will be performed a grand concert of Music by the best hands ... likewise the Dead March in "Saul" to be performed with sackbuts.'

Announcement of a benefit concert for the celebrated trumpet player Valentine Snow, for whom Handel wrote obbligato parts in his operas and oratorios, in *London Journal* (1741)

'Tromboni and double-drums are now so frequently used at the opera, oratorios, and in symphonies that they are become a nuisance to lovers of pure harmony and refined tones; for, in fact, the vibrations of these instruments produce noise, not musical sounds.'

Charles Burney, in Abraham Rees's *New Encyclopaedia* (1819)

'The trombones are extremely good. The first, Schrade ... is a most gifted player, a complete master of his instrument who makes light of the most formidable difficulties and produces a magnificent tone from the tenor trombone – I should rather say tones, for by some process not yet explained he can play three or four notes at the same time.... During a fantasia which he performed at a public concert in Stuttgart, Schrade paused at a pedal point and to the astonishment of all present sounded simultaneously the four notes of the chord of the dominant seventh in the key of B flat, pitched as follows: E flat, A, C, F. It is for the acousticians to account for this new phenomenon of natural resonance.'

The Memoirs of Hector Berlioz, translated and edited by **David Cairns** (1969)

'Once a troubled trombone-player approached [Toscanini] just before an opera performance and said that one of the low notes on his instrument would not sound. There was no time to get the trombone repaired or to borrow another. "What shall I do, maestro?" the player said nervously. Toscanini shut his eyes and seemed in deep thought. Then his eyes flashed open, and he smiled. "Don't worry", he said, "that note is not in tonight's opera."'

Howard Taubman *The Maestro: The Life of Arturo Toscanini* (1951)

Trumpet

For if the trumpet give an uncertain sound,
Who shall prepare himself to the battle?

1 Corinthians 14: 8

Be thou as lightning in the eyes of France;
For ere thou canst report I will be there,
The thunder of my cannon shall be heard:
So hence! Be thou the trumpet of our wrath.

William Shakespeare *King John*, Act III, scene ii (1596)

Make all our trumpets speak; give them all breath.
Those clamorous harbingers of blood and death.

William Shakespeare *Macbeth*, Act V, scene vi (1605)

They now to fight are gone,
Armour on armour shone,
Drum to drum did groan,
    To hear was wonder.
That with the cries they make
The very earth did shake,
Trumpet to trumpet spake,
    Thunder to thunder.

Michael Drayton (1562–1631) *Ballad of Agincourt*

At the round earth's imagined corners, blow
Your trumpets, angels; and arise, arise
From death, you numberless infinities
Of souls, and to your scattered bodies go. . . .

John Donne *Holy Sonnets* 7 (1633)

'My sword I give to him that shall succeed me in my pilgrimage, and my courage and skill to him that can get it. My marks and scars I carry with me, to be a witness for me that I have fought his battles who now will be my rewarder. When the day he must go hence was come, many accompanied him to the riverside, into which as he went he said: "Death, where is thy sting?" And as he went down deeper, he said: "Grave, where is thy victory?" So he passed over, and all the trumpets sounded for him on the other side.'

John Bunyan *The Pilgrim's Progress*, Part 2 (1678)

The trumpet's loud clangour
Excites us to arms,
With shrill notes of anger,
And mortal alarms.

John Dryden *A Song for St. Cecilia's Day* (1687)

'The silver, snarling trumpets 'gan to chide.'

John Keats *The Eve of St Agnes* (1818)

'When the tumpet sounds the signal of danger, man hastens to join his comrades, no matter what the cause that calls them to arms. He rushes into the thickest of the fight, and amid the uproar of battle regains confidence in himself and his powers.'

Alphonse Lamartine *Méditations poétiques* (1820)

I dimly guess what Time in mists confounds;
Yet ever and anon a trumpet sounds
From the hid battlements of Eternity;
Those shaken mists a space unsettle, then
Round the half-glimpsed turrets slowly wash again.

Francis Thompson *Hound of Heaven* (1893)

Now I am a tin whistle
Through which God blows,
And I wish to God I were a trumpet
– But why, God only knows.

John Collings Squire (1884–1958) *A Fresh Morning*

If after death, love, comes a waking,
And in their camp so dark and still
The men of dust hear bugles, breaking
Their halt upon the hill,

To me the slow and silver pealing
That then the last high trumpet pours
Shall softer than the dawn come stealing,
For, with its call, comes yours!

Herbert Trench (1865–1923) *I Heard a Soldier*

The Reverend Sydney Smith's idea of heaven was 'eating *pâtés de foie gras* to the sound of trumpets'.

Hesketh Pearson *The Smith of Smiths* (1934)

Vaughan Williams, Ralph
(1872–1958)

'... it is no exaggeration to say that the creation of a particular type of grey, reflective, English-landscape mood has outweighed the exigencies of symphonic form. To those who find this mood sympathetic, their intense and personal emotional reaction will more than compensate for the monotony of texture and the lack of form....'

Constant Lambert, of the *Pastoral Symphony*, in *Music Ho!* (1934)

'A pleasant trifle that sounds like Rimski-Korsakov with bowler, mackintosh and umbrella.'

Paul Henry Lang, of *The Wasps* Overture conducted by Sir Malcolm Sargent, in *the New York Herald Tribune*; quoted in **Charles Reid** *Malcolm Sargent: a Biography* (1968)

Verdi, Giuseppe (1813–1901)

'*Ernani* is the production of a young but prolific composer.... His greatest admirers claim for him the merit of entire originality: but in this they are really outstripping justice and discretion, since his real position and character as a composer may be fairly summed up in one sentence ... Verdi is another Donizetti.... Is this not praise enough for any young Italian, who neither seems to understand the scientific depths of German harmony, or the rapid expressions of the school of France? ... The music was characteristic by its easy, melodious flow.... Its inspiration rather that of champagne than of port or burgundy.'

Review of the first performance in London of *Ernani* on 8 March 1845, in *Pictorial Times*

'... the band commenced a lugubrious strain ... in the first scene there were countless chandeliers and a vulgar dance tune.... Then the amorous Duke made love to one Countess Ceprano, personated by a Miss Smythson (who seemed frightened out of her senses), her jealous husband looking daggers in the background.... The situation is highly dramatic, but with Verdi's inexpressive and frightfully ugly music ... it fell flat upon the audience ... nothing could possibly be better than the scenery, costumes etc. but we cannot set down this opera as a great success.... Our opinion of Signor Verdi's powers is well known, and as his present work is rather worse than better than his previous productions ... it will be unnecessary to enter into painful details.'

Review of a production of *Rigoletto* at Covent Garden, in the *Morning Post* (16 May 1853)

'*La Traviata* was a grand fiasco, and what is worse, they laughed. However, I am not disturbed about it. Am I wrong, or are they? I believe myself that the last word on *La Traviata* is not that of last night. They will see it again – and we shall see!'

Giuseppe Verdi, in a letter to a friend after the première of *La traviata* at Venice on 6 March 1853

'I have no love for useless things. Requiem Masses exist in plenty, plenty! It is useless to add one more to their number.'

Giuseppe Verdi, in a comment to the chief conductor at La Scala, Milan, who urged him to complete his Requiem in 1873

'I am not a knowledgeable composer. But I am a very experienced composer.'

Giuseppe Verdi

In *Aaron's Rod* the hero, Aaron Sisson, secretary to the Miners' Union at a colliery in the Midlands, leaves his wife and family and plays the flute in a London opera house. He is seen quite early in the novel playing in the orchestra in a production of Verdi's *Aida*:

'The singers were all colour-washed ... to a bright orange tint. The men had oblong dabs of black wool under their lower lip (which) shook and wagged to the singing.

The vulgar bodies of the fleshy women were unendurable.... Why were their haunches so prominent? ... their really expensive, brilliant clothing ... was *nearly* right – nearly splendid ... the leading tenor was the chief pain. He was large, stout, swathed in a cummerbund, and looked like a eunuch ... his mouth made a large coffin-shaped, yawning gap in his orange face, his little beard fluttered oddly, like a tail ... his abdomen shook as he caught his breath, the flesh of his fat naked arms swayed.'

D.H. Lawrence *Aaron's Rod* (1922)

'At last, at last the great day has come and gone, and Verdi has added the crown jewel to his diadem of triumphs.... From pit to dome, the immense auditorium was one mass of eager faces, sparkling eyes, brilliant toilettes, and splendid jewels.... La Scala is not alone in its nobility, its platea and boxes. Besides the celebrities here and there ... La Scala's real public is in the upper tiers, in pit, or lobbione.... They know La Scala and everything pertaining to it by heart; nine cases out of ten, they are better musicians than those in the band, better artists than those on the stage. They come to sit in judgement: to applaud or hiss, as they honestly feel; to lend their presence to the event of what is to them the entire world: the annual opening of a new opera, or a first night at their renowned opera-house; in short, they are a part of it. . . .

The scenery, costumes, choruses, and orchestra were nearly perfect; the cast was certainly weak. Victor Maurel is the only real artist in the opera, and he is a Frenchman. In voice, acting, appearance, and dress, he is the ideal of what any operatic artist should be, and the ideal of what any operatic Iago could be. He sang as even his best friends never dreamed he could sing, and his acting was the consummate work which we always have at his artistic hands. He entered at once into the fullest sympathies of the audience. . . . Iago even seems *a persona grata* to the public; the qualities which raise a thrill of horror in the righteous Anglo-Saxon are perceived by this susceptible nation with placid contentment and relief. His vileness, ruses and perfidy are accepted for their art, not their nature; his ingenious devices arouse heartfelt plaudits . . . never will you hear a gallery god in Italy express any disapprobation with a successful knave. . . . Iago is essentially Italian, not in the sense of vice, but of artistic villainy: he reasons from the personal standpoint, and his reasons find a universal echo in the land which gave birth to such a student of human nature as Macchiavelli. Otello, you will see, is an inferior creature, and plays an inferior part. . . .

. . . Tamagno, the tenor, looked and acted Otello, but he did not sing – he bleated. . . . Madama Panteleone (Desdemona) is an excellent person, but as Desdemona she ought to have been suppressed the night before at her dress rehearsal. Her voice is naturally fine and dramatic, but she has no more knowledge of the pure art of singing than I have of the real science of astronomy. She has a vile emission of tone in the medium open notes; the upper notes are clear, but rarely in tune. . . . In appearance Madame Panteleone is likewise unfortunate: she is short, slightly cross-eyed, and of a physical plainness. . . . She acted very well in the first and third acts, but not so well in the last. . . .

The ovations to Verdi and Boito reached the climax of enthusiasm. Verdi was presented with a silver album filled with autographs and cards of every citizen in Milan. He was called out twenty times . . . many wept. Verdi's carriage was dragged by citizens to the hotel.'

Account of the first performance of *Otello* at La Scala, Milan (5 Feb 1887) **Blanche Roosevelt** *Verdi: Milan and Otello* (1887)

'If this [Verdi's Requiem] is music more suitable for the theatre than the church, then so much the worse for the church.'

Charles Osborne *The Complete Operas of Verdi* (1969)

'. . . then came one of the great and rare moments when people and music become one. Without any preconcerted plan, by some inexplicable inspiration, there suddenly rose out of the monstrous soul of the multitude the chorus from *Nabucco* with which Giuseppe Verdi had become the voice of consolation and hope for his people, sixty years before – *Va, pensiero sull' ali dorate.'*

Franz Werfel, describing Verdi's funeral, in *Verdi* (1947)

'I am an arrogant and impatient listener; but in the case of a few composers, a very few, when I hear a work I do not like I am convinced it is my own fault. Verdi is one of these composers.'

Benjamin Britten, in *Opera* (Feb 1951)

Victoria, Queen (1819–1901)

'Princess Victoria's gift for languages was encouraged by her intense love of the opera and ballet. She learnt Italian under this stimulus and the pages of her Journal were spattered with operatic ejaculations, especially in moments of rage. It was through the opera, rather than formal education, that she saw into the world of art and poetry.'

Elizabeth Longford *Victoria R.I.* (1964)

Villa Lobos, Heitor (1887–1959)

'Why is it, that whenever I hear a piece of music I don't like, it's always by Villa Lobos?'

Igor Stravinsky

Viola

'The bull-fiddle players were solid men who played the notes set before them, however difficult, in a dogged and uncomplaining manner. . . . The cellists were also pretty reliable fellows, but in the viola section one began to encounter boozers, communists and even spiritualists.'

H.L. Mencken *The Tone Art* (1903)

Violin

Sharp violins proclaim
Their jealous pangs, and desperation,
Fury, frantic indignation,

Depth of pains, and height of passion,
For the fair, disdainful dame.

John Dryden *A Song for St. Cecilia's Day* (1687)

'Dr. Johnson was observed by a musical friend of his to be extremely inattentive at a concert whilst a celebrated solo player was running up the division and sub-division of notes upon his violin. His friend, to induce him to take greater notice of what was going on, told him how extremely difficult it was: "Difficult do you call it, sir?" replied the Doctor, "I wish it were impossible."'

William Seward *A Supplement to Seward's Anecdotes* (1795)

        The sly whoresons
Have got a speeding trick to lay down ladies;
A French song and a fiddle has no fellow.

William Shakespeare *Henry VIII*, Act I, scene iii (1613)

Is it not strange that sheeps' guts should hale souls out of men's bodies?

William Shakespeare *Much Ado About Nothing*, Act II, scene iii (1598)

'Violins are the lively, forward, importunate wits, that distinguish themselves by the flourishes of imagination, sharpness of repartee, glances of satire, and bear away the upper part in every consort.'
'When a man is not disposed to hear music, there is not a more disagreeable sound in harmony than that of the violin.'

Sir Richard Steele, in *The Tatler* (1 April 1710)

'. . . take the fiddle. It is a good sign, no doubt, that it is so much more generally practised than it used to be. But it is a terribly powerful instrument in neighbourhoods where only millionaires can afford to live in detached houses.'

George Bernard Shaw *Music in London 1890–94*, entry for 11 Jan 1893

'Music with dinner is an insult both to the cook and violinist.'

G.K. Chesterton, quoted in the *New York Times* (16 Nov 1967)

Virtuosos

My cup was filled with rapture to the brim
    When, night by night, – Ah, memory – how it haunts!
Music was poured by perfect ministrants
    By Hallé, Schumann, Piatti, Joachim!

Robert Browning *The Founder of the Feast* (1884)

Wagner, Richard (1813–83)

'One can't judge Wagner's opera *Lohengrin* after a first hearing, and I certainly don't intend hearing it a second time.'

Gioachino Rossini

'Wagner is obviously mad.'

Hector Berlioz

'Very commonplace, vulgar and uninteresting.'

Arthur Sullivan, of *Rienzi*; quoted in **Hesketh Pearson** *Gilbert and Sullivan* (1935)

'If this is the new religion I am far from practising it. . . . I raise my hand and swear *Non credo*.'

Hector Berlioz, of Wagnerism, in the *Journal des débats* (1860)

'. . . In order to become a radically healthy human being, I went two years ago to a Hydropathic Establishment; I was prepared to give up Art and everything if I could once more become a child of Nature. But, my good friend, I was obliged to laugh at my own *naiveté* when I found myself almost going mad. None of us will reach the promised land – we shall all die in the wilderness. Intellect is, as someone has said, a sort of disease; it is incurable. In the present conditions of life, Nature only admits of abnormalities. At the best we can only hope to be martyrs; to refuse this vocation is to put oneself in opposition to the possibilities of life. For myself, I can no longer exist except as an artist; since I cannot compass love and life, all else repels me, or only interests me in so far as it has a bearing on Art. The result is a life of torment, but it is the only possible life. Moreover, some strange experiences have come to me through my works. When I think of the pain and discomfort which are now my chronic condition, I cannot but feel that my nerves are completely shattered: but marvellous to relate, on occasion, and under a happy stimulus, these nerves do wonders for me; a clearness of insight comes to me, and I experience a receptive and creative activity such as I have never known before. After this, can I say that my nerves are shattered? Certainly not. But I must admit that the normal condition of my temperament – as it has been developed through circumstances – is a state of exultation, whereas calm and repose is its abnormal condition. The fact is, it is only when I am "beside myself" that I become my real self, and feel well and happy. . . .'

Richard Wagner, in a letter to August Roeckel, 26 Jan 1854

'With mighty exulting tones the enchantingly passionate Motive of Love's Rapture sounds after the duet and the powerful Siegfried-Motive then relieves the Greeting Motive with gentler motion.

Compassion with Siegfried's unhappy parents was the origin of her pure, holy love for the son, and thus Brünnhilde's touching air ends with the reception of the death-song and her justification-melody. In Siegfried's answer the excited figure of Love's confusion soon breaks forth and grows into f., when the impetuous youth ardently implores her: "Unfix my manhood from might of thy fetters", and then longingly stops with the Motive of Renunciation: "gives it to freedom again". . . . Brünnhilde sees her horse (with the gaily jumbling Walküren-Motive) in the near fir-gove, and this view makes her think sadly of her former godship, which is now to be lost altogether in the fervour of man's earthly love . . . she once more opposes him gravely and solemnly with the Walhall-Motive: "Holy went I from Walhall!" Then his love ominously takes the Motive of the World's Heritage into its service and turns it from the symbol of the highest heroism into the charming expression of sensual love's desire: "A woman awaken to be!" But above it the gloomy spectre of the *curse* rises menacingly. . . .'

Hans von Wolzogen, describing the awakening of the sleeping Brünnhilde by Siegfried in Act III of *Siegfried*, in *A Guide Through the Music of Richard Wagner's 'The Ring of the Nibelung'* (1882)

During a rehearsal of *Die Götterdämmerung* at Covent Garden, when the Curse motif recurred (not for the first time) Sir Thomas Beecham exclaimed: 'We've been rehearsing for two hours – and we're still playing the same bloody tune!'

Charles Reid *Beecham: an Independent Biography* (1961)

'*Parsifal* – the kind of opera that starts at six o'clock and after it has been going three hours, you look at your watch and it says 6.20.'

David Randolph, quoted in the *Frank Muir Book* (1976)

'It was just as boring as every other production of *Lohengrin* I have ever seen, but that was inevitable, because *Lohengrin* simply happens to be a bore. The important thing is that it was not *offensively* boring. No Marxist half-wit of a producer equipped the grail knight with a homburg hat. Instead the radiant hero was properly attired in shining armour. His long aluminium combat jacket made his legs look like a hamster's, but at least he wasn't riding a penny-farthing.'

Clive James, on the Bavarian State Opera production of *Lohengrin* shown on BBC television, in *The Observer* (17 Dec 1978)

'Wagner held to an aesthetic standard, relating all the conflicts of the age to himself and his work, he gave utterance to reaction and revolution, continuity and innovation, the real and the ideal.'

Martin Gregor-Dellin *Richard Wagner* (1983)

'Wagner's music is better than it sounds.'

Bill Nye (Edgar Wilson Nye), American humorist and journalist (1850–96)

'His doctrine, anarchistically tinged, of regeneration through the communal experience of art in a post revolutionary society turned into an inflated pseudo-religion that offered an ersatz salvation. Ambivalence and incoherence transcended through an extraordinary musical intelligence were what he was about.'

John Roselli, in *The Guardian* (2 June 1983)

'The quality in Wagner's music which attracts his admirers is the same quality which repels his detractors. It is not merely that the emotion it expresses is overwhelmingly human.... Wagner's music is not only very human, but human in a very earthy way. Against this earthiness there is set a capacity for exaltation not only of the senses but of the spirit too. In other words, Wagner touches the depths and he touches the heights. He covers the span of human experience with an impartial zest and relish which is at the very least Rabelaisian, and which those who admire him as much as I do would call Faustian.'

Robert Donington *Wagner's 'Ring' and its Symbols: the Music and the Myth* (1963)

Weber, Carl Maria von (1786–1826)

'... the complicated nature of some parts of the drama entitle it to the most favourable consideration, while the exertions which have been made in its production are highly praiseworthy.... When the witches and devils, and toads, and skeletons get well into their several parts, we have no doubt they will make very respectable beasts; and as soon as the fireworks are sensible of the manner in which they ought to go off, the scene of the incantation will be a very powerful one of its kind.'

Review of the first London performance of *Der Freischütz*, on 22 July 1824 at the Lyceum, in *The Times*; quoted in **Denis Arundel** *The Critic at the Opera* (1957)

'Never again has a German composer poured into such sweet and at the same time such virile tones the deep-rooted romanticism in the German heart, with its woods and elves, its water sprites and sorcerers, its moonlight and its Puckish humour.... If all German culture were buried and nothing were left but Weber's three overtures and the "Invitation to the Dance", the discoverers a few thousand years hence would be bound to conclude that this lost people must have been enchanting.'

Emil Ludwig *The Germans*(1942)

Webern, Anton (1883–1945)

'It is a profoundly tragic expression which builds inexorably from piece to piece forming ultimately a hexagonal unity of dark, daemonic power, terribly contained ... it compresses into its brooding strength a feeling akin to that evoked by some of the best sections of Berg's later *Lulu* orchestral suite. It breathes the same poisoned air which we have learned to know as our very own in the twentieth century and it reminds us overpoweringly that man is still a tragic creature whatever his source – whether divine or not – but above all, tragic. In other words, Webern's Opus 6 speaks truth.'

George Rochberg, review of Webern's *Six Pieces*Opus 6, in *Notes*[of the Music Library Association, Washington, DC], **16** (Fall 1958–9)

Writing About Music

'Aside from purely technical analysis, nothing can be *said*about music, except when it is bad; when it is good, one can only listen and be grateful.'

W.H. Auden Foreword to *A Certain World*(1981)

Zither

'The music of the zither, flute and the lyre enervates the mind.'

Ovid *Remedorium amoris*(c16 BC)

Index

The index lists sections of the book (in **bold** type) together with the authors or sources for the quotations.

151

Index

Index

Published by
Longman Group Limited,
Longman House, Burnt Mill, Harlow,
Essex CM20 2JE, England
and Associated Companies throughout the
world.

First published 1984

British Library Cataloguing in
Publication Data

Giddings, Robert
  Pocket companion guide to musical
  quotations.—(Longman pocket
  companion series)
  1. Music—Quotations, maxims, etc.
  I. Title
  082 ML66

  ISBN 0-582-55688-0

Acknowledgements

We are grateful to the following for permission to
reproduce copyright material:
The author, Alan Bold for his poem 'Music' ©
Alan Bold (1984); Michael Grieve on behalf of the
estate of Hugh MacDiarmid, for the poems
'Bagpipe Music' and 'Plaited Like the
Generations of Men' from *The Complete Poems of
Hugh MacDiarmid* edited by M. Grieve and Dr. W.
Aitken (pub O'Keefe); Macdonald Publishers and
the author, Alan Bold for the poem 'In This
Corner' from *Selected Poems 1963–1983* © Alan
Bold (1983); the author, F. Scott Monument and
The Scotsman Publications Ltd for the poem 'The
Muzak Snob' from *The Weekend Scotsman.*

While every effort has been made to clear
permissions with copyright holders, this has not
always been possible. Copyright holders to
whom this applies should contact the Publisher.

Set in 7½/8½ Linotron Palatino
Printed and bound in Great Britain by
William Clowes Limited,
Beccles and London